AF846391

WORK FAME

WORK FAME

GET THE PROJECTS, PROMOTIONS AND PERKS YOU DESERVE

LEANNE HUGHES

WILEY

First published 2027 by John Wiley & Sons Australia, Ltd

ISBN: 978-1-394-42630-0

NATIONAL LIBRARY OF AUSTRALIA

A catalogue record for this book is available from the National Library of Australia

Registered Office
John Wiley & Sons Australia, Ltd. Level 4, 600 Bourke Street, Melbourne, VIC 3000, Australia

For details of our global editorial offices, customer services, and more information about Wiley products visit us at www.wiley.com.

Wiley also publishes its books in a variety of electronic formats and by print-on-demand. Some content that appears in standard print versions of this book may not be available in other formats.

Cover Image: © Download Now./Adobe Stock
Cover design by Wiley
Author photo: Jason Malouin
Illustrations by Jade Miller

Set in 11.5/16.5 pts and Warnock Pro by Straive, Chennai, India.
Printed and bound by CPI Group (UK) Ltd, Croydon, CR0 4YY

C9781394426300_040926

The manufacturer's authorized representative according to the EU General Product Safety Regulation is Wiley-VCH GmbH, Boschstr. 12, 69469 Weinheim, Germany, e-mail: Product_Safety@wiley.com.

For Milo Fong, our rescue dog in the sky, who showed me that a happy smile and relentless enthusiasm for life will open every door that matters to you.

Contents

Foreword

by Alan Weiss

'Fame' is hardly a new concept — despite Andy Warhol's famous observation that 'In the future, everyone will be famous for 15 minutes.'

The origins, in fact, date back to the early 13th Century and Middle English, where the term meant 'character and renown attributed to someone.' The biblical concept was about 'the quality of a person's trustworthiness, integrity, and spiritual weight.'

So we're dealing with an eons-old concept that is quite respectable and desirable. Yet the immediate importance of Leanne Hughes's approach is that she's aligned the historical importance with contemporary reality.

Fame is our personal brand. And while, formally, one might describe a 'brand' with the great pomp of 'consistent quality represented to customers,' I'll use a more pragmatic definition: 'A brand is how people think about you when you're not around.'

Hence, *Work Fame* is the rationale and, indeed, *urgency* for others to know of your presence, your contributions, and your worth. And what I love about Leanne's approach is that she positions the goal as perfectly reasonable and achievable whether in a long-term tenure in an organization, in an entrepreneurial and personal venture, in both professional and personal endeavors.

She consistently provides the rationale, the social proof, and the ease of use for the principles to achieve such a splendid reputation of substance, whether in a department, an organisation, a municipality, or globally. (I know Leanne because we both have a global 'work fame.') Merely her example of 'contribution, conversations, and coverage' is an excellent approach to organise your 'work fame' game plan.

I urge you to take a marker, some adhesive notes, and/or a recorder to remember and apply her ideas. Work Fame is entirely possible for you to improve your work and your life, and I know that because Leanne's been there and done that!

—Alan Weiss, PhD
Author of *Fearless Leadership* and over
50 other books on human performance

Introduction

It's time to claim your Work Fame

Being famous isn't all it's cracked up to be. Mentions in gossip columns and attacks from keyboard warriors? No thanks. But that's celebrity fame; I'm talking about something else.

If I asked you whether you'd like to be recognised for your work, travel to interesting places, meet great people, maybe skip a queue (okay, I might be over-promising there) or be thought of first when an exciting project comes up, I already know the answer. You want what fame delivers. I'm here to tell you that you can have the perks, places, people and parties, without the paparazzi. You can have Work Fame.

> **Work Fame** (noun): **A reputation that opens doors before you knock and attracts the right opportunities. 'She has serious Work Fame. The GM of Americas recognised her at a conference and said, "I've heard great things about you".'**

The word 'fame' comes from the Latin word *fama,* which means 'rumour' and 'report'—basically, 'to be talked about'. To be talked about, you need to have something *worth* talking about. That's what this book covers—doing work worth noticing, and then making sure it gets noticed.

Work Fame helps you become known for the right work, by the right people, before the right opportunities appear.

It's about building a reputation that's strong across your organisation, your industry and—if you want it—the world.

If you're reading this and thinking Work Fame sounds like humble-bragging or sharing that you're 'thrilled' on LinkedIn, it couldn't be further from that. Stick with me.

Have you ever had the feeling that you've poured your heart and soul into your work, delivered something truly exceptional, and then ... crickets? Meanwhile, someone else, perhaps not even doing work that's objectively 'better', seems to effortlessly capture all the attention and accolades. It's frustrating, right? But it's more common than you think. Dina Kamel's 2025 research on visibility versus performance shows that our organisational systems often, and quite unintentionally, reward those who are good at being visible, rather than those who are delivering behind the scenes.[1]

So, if you've ever felt like your good work isn't speaking for itself, this book will show you why that happens—and how to make sure your contributions are seen, valued and celebrated.

Why should you become Work Famous?

Work Fame is a serious career asset that gives you options. In a world where job security is shaky and AI is absorbing more of the predictable, transactional work, your Work Fame is your career insurance. Your reputation travels with you through every restructure, every leadership change and every industry shift. The skills you build by becoming Work Famous are transferrable and work across every level and industry.

Being Work Famous also leads to living a great life. The internet seems to be full of content celebrating quiet quitting and doing the bare minimum — as though working to half your potential is something to aspire to. Gosh, it's not. We have *one life* and it is meant to be lived to the full!

When you have that energy at work, it spills over into everything else. Gallup's research across millions of workers found that people who are engaged at work are significantly more likely to be thriving in their lives overall — not just professionally, but also across their health, relationships and sense of purpose.[2] When you feel like you are contributing meaningfully and being recognised for it, you can unlock some genuinely extraordinary life experiences — including opportunities, access, travel and moments that money alone cannot buy.

Who this book is for (and who it isn't for)

As you read through (or, like I usually do, skim and highlight) these pages, you will learn how to make your work visible, share your potential more broadly and be recognised for the efforts you're already putting in.

I'll show you how to use the three Work Fame Spotlights of Contribution, Conversations and Coverage to attract the opportunities that make your work (and life) genuinely exciting.

This book is for you if:

- you feel like you're being overlooked at work despite doing excellent work
- you want practical tools for reaching out to people, speaking up in rooms and making your work visible without coming across as pushy, performative or overly self-interested
- you wince at the phrase 'personal branding' but know that if nothing changes, you will keep doing solid work without the recognition, influence or opportunities to match
- you want some encouragement and a framework for building your profile within your organisation and your industry.

This book is not for you if work is a place where you show up, collect a pay cheque and leave. Nothing is wrong with that, but everything in this book requires you to care about your work and want more from it.

It is also not for you if you want recognition without doing the work or would sacrifice other people in the process of getting ahead. Everything in this book is built on a foundation of service. And that foundation shows up in a simple but telling way: the questions you ask yourself.

The questions running through your head shape how you show up at work. They influence whether people experience you as someone they trust and want to work with, or as someone who is trying to get ahead.

The following table shows the difference.

Questions asked by self-promoters versus Work Famous people

Self-promoter questions	Work Famous questions
Who is watching me work?	How can I be useful?
How can I get credit for this?	What problems can I solve?
What will get me the most likes?	Where can I contribute my unique skills?

Essentially, Work Famous people ask questions to create value for others. If you're honest, you will likely recognise yourself in both columns at different times. That's normal. The point is to notice which questions are driving your behaviour most often.

A good reputation is built less through chasing attention and more through being useful, solving problems and contributing where it counts. That's the mindset behind this book.

Here is something counterintuitive before we go any further. I want you to have zero expectations of reward. Don't read this thinking, *If I do* x, *I will get* y. The paradox of Work Fame is that it works best when you're not keeping score. If you do everything in this book and nothing externally changes, you will still be a better professional, a better colleague, and a more interesting person to be around. Anything above that is a bonus.

How I became a work celebrity

The seed for this book was planted years ago, when I was six months into a new role with a global mining company. On paper, it was my dream job. In reality, every Sunday evening my stomach would clench, and I'd feel a sense of dread about going into the office on Monday morning.

I felt completely unseen and underutilised — spending most of my time at a screen, pinging and emailing people. I was delivering on my job description, but it felt flat. I honestly thought, *There's got to be more to life than this!*

I looked around and could see some bright pockets of goodness — colleagues around me were travelling, leading projects and getting pulled into opportunities that looked far more interesting than anything coming my way.

One afternoon, while scrolling job ads on the train home and seriously considering a move, a colleague said something I have never forgotten. 'Leanne, the grass isn't greener on the other side. It's just another shade of brown.' I laughed and asked him to repeat it, thinking, *This really isn't an inspiring TED Talk.* 'Shade of brown?' So demotivational.

But when I let that quote wash over me, I realised there could be some truth to it. Maybe the problem wasn't the job, the company or the lack of opportunity. I could leave my job and hope for a brighter future. Or maybe I could try to turn things around.

I had assumed that good work would speak for itself. But in a big organisation, it often doesn't. I was doing strong work for an audience of one, my manager, while opportunities were being shaped by relationships I hadn't built.

That realisation changed everything. This wasn't about finding my dream job. It was about (as corny as it sounds) making my job a dream. I had more agency than I thought.

So, I started experimenting. I volunteered for projects that put me in front of different leaders. I went up to Level 5 on Friday afternoons for the social club drinks, even when I barely knew anyone there. I started hosting 'lunch and learns' to share practical tips based on the questions I kept getting in my role.

People started asking me to be involved in things I hadn't applied for and, 18 months later, I had hosted leadership sessions across Canada, Indonesia, Mongolia and Australia. I moderated our organisation's Global Town Hall, interviewing our executive leadership team in front of 10 000 colleagues.

These days, I'm a keynote speaker and consultant, advising small and large organisations, teams and leaders around the world across many different industries. I've partnered with my favourite authors on events and workshops (pinch me!) and interviewed the world's greatest thought leaders on my podcast.

I wake up every day and can't believe how lucky I am to be able to use my strengths to do this work.

You can have that feeling every day, too.

Why does Work Fame matter now?

Job security is shakier than it used to be, industries are changing quickly and AI is swallowing more of the easy-to-replace stuff. If your value only lives in tasks that can be automated, templated or quietly absorbed into someone else's role, you're more exposed than you think.

Having Work Fame makes you easier to remember, easier to recommend and harder to overlook, and it helps people associate your name with good judgement, initiative, energy, trust and ideas — all the things that are much harder to automate and far more likely to open doors.

It's time to claim your Work Fame.

How to use this book

This book is written for busy people who would rather try something today than read about mindset for another 100 pages. To get an idea of the overall system, I suggest reading from start to finish and trying some of the activities as you go. The concepts are shared in bite-sized scenes (chapters) that build on each other.

Throughout the book, I refer to the three Work Fame spotlights:

1. *Contribution:* This is about doing great work and making sure it can be seen.
2. *Conversations:* This spotlight is about building relationships, trust and access over time.
3. *Coverage:* This is about sharing your point of view so your reputation can travel further than you do.

When all three spotlights are bright, opportunities start moving in your direction. Once you have more of an idea of which area might need the most work for you, you can focus in on that particular spotlight.

Throughout the scenes, I've included plenty of activities, tips and real-life examples from me to help you apply the information to your own situation. As you read, you'll also meet people who have built their own Work Fame in different ways. These people include executive leaders, graduates, consultants, managers and professionals across a range of industries. I've included their stories because no single Work Fame personality type exists, and I want you to see yourself in these pages. At the end of the book, you can also find a 90-day Work Fame action plan, and some 'quick fix' actions for each of the Work Fame scenes.

If you lead a team, read this book twice: once for yourself, and once for the people whose work deserves to travel further. The spotlights don't just apply to individuals; teams and organisations can be work famous, too.

And if you're still looking for more, you'll find extra resources, scripts, templates and tools for free at **getworkfame.com/start**.

Good on you for picking up this book. Now let's get you the projects, promotions and perks you deserve.

Scene 1

The three Work Fame spotlights and the Walk of Fame

I want you to imagine that your career runs on three spotlights. Each one lights up a different part of your reputation. Together, they determine how far your Work Fame travels. When all three Work Fame spotlights are bright, opportunities start moving in your direction.

Let's look at these three spotlights in a little more detail, before considering how you can create your own Walk of Fame.

Spotlight one: Contribution

Contribution relates to yourself and your relationship with your work. It is the quality of what you do, the results you deliver, the expertise you build and the standard people can count on when something important lands on your desk. This spotlight begins with you and is the foundation on which everything else rests. Without Contribution, nothing else in this book matters.

However, Contribution is also the spotlight that can steal the show. You might find yourself pouring everything into being excellent, reliable, thorough and indispensable within your immediate role, and then wondering why nobody outside your team knows you exist.

Contribution is about doing great work and also making sure it can be seen. In their study of passive 'face time', Kimberly Elsbach, Dan Cable and Jeffrey Sherman found that simply being seen at work shaped how employees were judged, even when no interaction took place. They identified two forms of visibility: being seen during normal working hours, which led observers to infer that an employee was dependable, and being seen outside normal hours, which led observers to infer that an employee was committed. Importantly, their experimental study suggested that these judgements were made spontaneously — people drew conclusions about reliability and commitment without necessarily intending to or realising they had done so.[3]

The most dangerous assumption you can make is that Contribution alone is enough.

Spotlight two: Conversations

Conversations build your relationships with other people. The Conversations spotlight is about the people who know you, trust you and would advocate for you if someone asked. These people include your manager, your peers, the people in other functions you have built a genuine connection with, the senior leader who remembers the question you asked at the town hall and the industry contact who thinks of you when an opportunity comes up.

This spotlight gets brighter in two ways:

1. *One-to-one conversations:* This includes reaching out to people, following up, staying on their radar and being someone they are genuinely glad to hear from.
2. *One-to-many conversations:* This could be hosting meetings, running 'lunch and learns', moderating panels, facilitating workshops, contributing at town halls and creating rooms where people experience you in action.

Spotlight three: Coverage

Coverage is your relationship with the wider world. It is how your reputation scales across your industry, and how your ideas travel further than you do.

Coverage looks like sharing a point of view on LinkedIn, posting about what you're learning, actively contributing to an industry or a professional body, speaking at an event, recording a podcast, or simply making your thinking more visible in ways other people can find, share and remember.

This is the spotlight that's easy to pass on, because it feels uncomfortable, self-promotional or unnecessary. But when attention is scattered and AI is making generic output easier than ever, your thinking, judgement, lived experience and point of view matter more than ever.

The Spotlight System

This might seem like a lot, but you don't need to fix everything at once — and you're probably already doing some of these things. You just may not be doing them strategically yet.

The great news is that the spotlights illuminate each other. Here's how:

- *Contribution lights up Coverage:* When you're doing good work, solving problems and learning useful things, you're creating meaningful experiences you can share. You have something to talk about, write about, teach or share.
- *Conversations light up Contribution:* When you're in conversations (meeting new people, catching up with existing contacts or hosting events), you're hearing things that change how you think. Someone mentions a problem you could help with, for example, or a peer shares an approach you had never considered.
- *Coverage lights up Conversation:* When you share your thinking, people have a reason to notice you. They message you. They forward your post. Your ideas begin travelling

beyond your immediate circle, opening conversations with people, opportunities and possibilities you may never have imagined.

The challenge is keeping all three spotlights lit up. Coverage dims if you stop sharing, Conversations fade if you stop reaching out and Contribution becomes invisible if you stop doing the work worth noticing.

Check where your light is strongest

Before we go further, let's see where you are right now.

For each statement, give yourself a score from one ('not at all') to five ('strongly agree'). (Use a rating of three for 'somewhat agree'.)

Contribution:

- 'I know what I want to be famous for at work.'
- 'People outside my immediate team know what I do.' (Bonus points if they can describe why it matters.)
- 'I can point to outcomes, not just activity, when I describe my work.'
- 'In the past 90 days, I have created, improved or solved something that added visible value.'

Conversations:

- 'I regularly speak with people beyond my immediate team.'
- 'In the past month, I have reached out to someone without needing anything from them.'
- 'People come to me to ask, "Who should I talk to about this?"'
- 'I have hosted, co-hosted or actively contributed to a meeting, event, discussion or room where people can experience how I think and work.'

Coverage:

- 'In the past month, I shared an idea, an update or a piece of thinking that someone outside my team could see.'
- 'I am not waiting until I feel perfectly ready to share useful ideas.'
- 'Someone I have never met has contacted me because of something I wrote, posted or presented.'
- 'If someone looked me up tomorrow, they could find evidence of my thinking, voice, value or contribution.'

Which spotlight needs to shine brighter?

Add up your scores for each spotlight to determine your total out of a possible 20 per spotlight.

Here's how to read your results:

- *16 to 20:* This spotlight is strong and it's already doing work for you. People can see it. It's helping your reputation travel.
- *11 to 15:* This spotlight is switched on, but patchy. It shows up sometimes, but not consistently enough to really carry you.
- *6 to 10:* This spotlight is dim. It's there, but it's not doing much for you yet.
- *0 to 5:* This spotlight is off. Whatever you're doing in this area, it's happening in the shadows.

Now look at your three scores together. You're not trying to get perfect marks across the board but are instead looking for the pattern.

If one spotlight is much higher than the others, that's probably the area that has been carrying your career so far. It's your go-to, the place where you naturally put your effort. That's useful to know, but it can also become a trap.

If one spotlight is clearly lower than the others, that's where you should start focusing your efforts to make a dramatic improvement.

If all three scores are low, it doesn't mean you're bad at your job or behind everyone else. It usually means you've been focused on doing the work rather than building a reputation around it, which is very normal. It also means you have a lot of room for things to shift quickly once you start being more deliberate.

If your scores across spotlights are similar, ask yourself, 'Which spotlight, if I lit it up, would make the biggest difference the fastest?' Pick one spotlight and go all in on it for the next 90 days to create a bright spot.

Quick tip: If you're not sure where to start, try either hosting something (a lunch and learn, a roundtable, a coffee catch-up with someone outside your team) to illuminate your Conversations spotlight or sharing one idea publicly each week to get your Coverage spotlight moving.

A note before you dive in

Each scene ahead is packed with practical ideas, exercises and examples. However, this isn't a checklist where you tick off every item and graduate with a certificate in Work Fame. What I've provided is more like a menu. Some ideas will land immediately and feel like they were written for you. Others won't fit your role, your industry or your personality, and that's fine. Skip them.

Pick the actions that make sense for your situations and feel doable, and start there. You can always come back for more.

Let's see how these spotlights can map across someone's career, in the first of many case studies I've included through this book. You've likely heard of (or seen) Hollywood's 'Walk of Fame' — the stretch of footpath along Hollywood Boulevard in Los Angeles, United States, where more than 2700 stars are embedded in the ground. Each one carries the name of someone the entertainment industry has decided to honour. Tourists fly from all over the world to find their favourite celebrity's name, crouch down and take a photo with it. I've borrowed from this tradition in creating my own Walk of Fame in the case studies included here.

Work Fame in action

Charlotte Evans

Charlotte Evans is Director of Global Customer Advocacy at Coursera, a leading global online learning platform. In her role, Charlotte supports clients across multiple regions and industries. Not too many years ago, she was working at universities in Shanghai and Singapore, supporting first-generation students and wondering how to create that kind of impact at a much bigger scale. Now, she delivers keynote speeches around the world, participates in major customer partner conversations, and attends meetings with senior corporate and government leaders. Best of all? She helped design this role herself.

Charlotte is a great example of how the three spotlights feed each other when you shine them deliberately.

When she first joined Coursera, Charlotte found herself at the centre of a platform bug. Engineers started talking to her about Python, APIs, JavaScript and SQL, and she quickly realised that to keep up, she would need a crash course in the technical world. She started taking Coursera courses on weekends and eventually completed more than 75 of them. She wanted to become, in her words, 'dangerous; not dangerous in a bad way, but able to collaborate properly with technical people, understand what was going on and contribute something useful'.

That investment changed the quality of every interaction she had across the business. When she went to engineers or product teams with a request, she could scope it properly, tell the difference between a small ask and a giant one, and show up with a rough starting point rather than a vague brief. That cast light on her Contribution spotlight—and engineers noticed. Over time, they started coming to her too, asking her to test ideas with customers and help shape the story around what they had built.

As her credibility grew, so did the quality of her Conversations spotlight. Charlotte started noticing that customers were increasingly talking about skills-based organisations, workforce agility and talent mobility. The market conversation was shifting, and both Charlotte and her peers saw the opportunity for Coursera to play a role in that discussion. She could have just observed that and moved on but, instead, she started digging into it. She researched the space, built out a point of view,

(*continued*)

created slides, and tested her thinking in customer conversations and on stage.

She thought creating a dedicated role around this work might be worthwhile, but she knew she couldn't make that happen alone. She needed people inside the organisation who understood the business case for it. So, she spent about a year cultivating those relationships—one mentor was arranged through her boss; another she initiated by reaching out directly.

Charlotte was strategic about how she used those conversations. She shared with her mentors (and others in the business) what she was noticing in the market, tested her ideas with them, asked for their perspective and let the case build gradually through conversation rather than trying to sell it in a single meeting.

By the time a global role started to take shape, it was more of a shared conclusion that Charlotte was the obvious choice for the role.

Finally, the Coverage spotlight.

Charlotte posts on LinkedIn and she's intentional about how she shows up there. She stays within Coursera's brand principles, but she writes in her own voice. 'If it doesn't sound like me, I don't post it', she said. If marketing gives her a link for something to promote, she'll use it, but she'll write her own take on why it matters.

Her first speaking opportunity for Coursera came because she said yes before she felt ready. She was in Florida for a friend's wedding when someone from marketing asked if anyone happened to be nearby to cover an ATD conference. Charlotte volunteered. Afterwards, she turned that one yes into a repeatable system: she started checking in with marketing every six months to learn when speaker slots were being decided, set calendar reminders to follow up and positioned herself before opportunities were allocated.

Over time, her visible thinking started creating its own momentum. An industry content partner, Star Weaver, had been quietly following her posts on AI and workforce transformation and invited her to keynote their virtual conference.

Inside Coursera, senior leaders began asking her to meet with important contacts, including a deputy prime minister, the CEO of a major Brazilian partner organisation, and other high-level stakeholders visiting headquarters.

'There is an element of it still feeling really uncomfortable to post pictures of myself on stage', she said. 'It feels oddly self-promotional. But when people see me presenting, I hope it helps them visualise me presenting at one of their events too.'

Charlotte is the first to say that putting yourself out there feels a little awkward. She's also proof of what happens when you do it anyway.

The Walk of Fame

Now I have a different version of the Walk of Fame — one you can do on the daily, and which involves you and your local footpath.

This practice starts with something you probably already do most days — going for a walk. Walking is one of the best things you can do for yourself. It's good for your health and your nervous system, and you can do it anywhere in the world. But every walk is also your chance to practise the skills that sit underneath everything in this book, including making an approach, smiling, saying hello, and being visible and out in the world. It's also your chance to put in place one thing that will support all the strategies: your willingness to initiate. Work Fame rewards people who make the first move.

When you walk anywhere, you can choose between two types of walks:

1. *The Walk of Tame:* This is your regular walk. Despite what my job might suggest, I'm not someone who wants to chat all day. A lot of my work involves being switched on and communicating constantly, so when I head out in the morning, I love plugging in my AirPods, throwing on a podcast or a playlist, and tuning everything else out. I keep my head down and walk at a steady pace with a fixed destination (and then upload photos of my walk to Strava). It's restorative and I recommend it.

2. *The Walk of Fame:* This one's a little different. You're not plugged in with music or distractions. You're looking around,

noticing the little things, such as birds screeching (which I heard this morning), and are more aware of your own thoughts. But the thing that makes it a Walk of Fame is one small but brave act: you say hi to the strangers you pass.

Most of us move through our working lives a bit like the Walk of Tame—our focus is narrow and internal. We're plugged into our own to-do list, our own team and our own metrics. As shown in the following table, when we take the Walk of Fame approach, our attention, engagement and purpose are different.

The Walk of Tame versus the Walk of Fame

Focus	Walk of Tame	Walk of Fame
Attention	Internal	External
Engagement	Plugged in, tuning everything else out	Saying hi to strangers
Purpose	Recharge and restore	Build micro-courage through small brave acts
Work parallel	Doing your job well within your own bubble	Looking up and connecting beyond your immediate circle

The Walk of Fame asks you to look up—pay attention to what's going on around you and engage with people you would not necessarily see cross your path often.

When you're on your Walk of Fame, you're away from your screen and you're practising two things at once: the attention to notice what's around you and the courage to make an approach. These skills are foundational. You can't create opportunities you haven't seen, and you can't take them if the discomfort of putting yourself forward stops you before you start.

Resting your rejection muscle

Saying hi to someone on the footpath creates a moment of vulnerability. You make eye contact and put a small, unasked-for piece of yourself out there. Sometimes — often, actually — people don't respond the way you hoped.

This morning, an elderly gentleman walked straight past my greeting without acknowledging it. For a couple of seconds, that warm rush of social discomfort washed over me. Did I do something wrong? Is my face broken? The good news is I was able to literally walk that feeling off.

And that's the gift of practising this outside, where the stakes are basically zero. The moment you decide to ask a senior leader for a coffee, raise your hand at a town hall or host that first panel, you will feel a version of that same discomfort. But you will have practised it and become more accustomed to it.

Practising while walking also sharpens your 'approach' skills. When someone's headed your way, you can start to notice your body language. You need eye contact for your greeting to land, your voice needs to project rather than hiding behind a morning muffle and, yes, a smile helps. These are the mechanics of how people warm to you and your ideas, practised in a context where nobody's keeping score.

One last thing to keep in mind: this isn't about getting a 'hello' back. That's a bonus. Go in with no expectations of a response.

What this looks like at work

Of course, the Walk of Fame doesn't have to stay on the footpath — your walk into work is a great time to give this a go, too.

Here's how you can adapt the Walk of Fame for your office commute:

- Take your headphones out before you hit the lobby and say good morning to the person on reception.
- Sit somewhere different for a change.
- Stop by someone's office when you walk past and say hello.
- Take the lift to another level and see who's around.

Building your pronoia engine

To keep showing up like that — saying hello to strangers on the footpath or putting your hand up at work when every instinct tells you to stay quiet — you need a specific kind of belief. It's called *pronoia,* coined by sociologist Fred Goldner in 1982 as the opposite of *paranoia* — the belief that the world is quietly conspiring in your favour.

Here's how the two belief systems work in practice:

- *Paranoia says:* 'They haven't replied because they hate my idea.'
- *Pronoia says:* 'They haven't replied because they're busy, or because the timing isn't right, or because they're working out what to do next.'

Working on your pronoia has flow-on benefits, including helping to increase your optimism. And psychologist Suzanne Segerstrom's research on optimism suggests that optimistic people don't just *feel* better but also tend to *do* better, because they persist longer, notice more options and approach people with an energy that makes help more likely. In a ten-year study following law students, Segerstrom found that the more optimistic first-year students earned significantly more money a decade later, because they positioned themselves to recognise and act on possibilities that others walked straight past.[4]

In short, pronoia and optimism mean you see the possibilities, not the problems.

Lochie McCabe is a good example of pronoia in action. He was a graduate mechanical engineer I once worked alongside. One day he showed up to work wearing a tie. That doesn't sound like much, except nobody at that company wore ties.

'It was, in a fun way, a bit of a statement piece', he told me. 'And then I thought, *Actually, this would be a good way to get noticed in the business*. It was just a fun way to stand out.'

His GM noticed first, loved it, and started wearing a tie too. Then it spread. A few months later, the Assets team on Level 8 were wearing ties every Tuesday.

When I asked where he got the courage, Lochie said he'd been practising since high school: putting his hand up, asking questions and going against the grain when it felt right.

'The upside of sticking your neck out is tenfold', he said. 'The downside is a bit of embarrassment. But no-one thinks about you for as long as you think they do.'

Lochie's tie was his Walk of Fame moment, because it had everything to do with his willingness to initiate, the belief that it would land well, and the acceptance that if it didn't, he'd survive. The worst-case scenario was a few seconds of discomfort. Lochie is now a leader at that organisation, and President of the Young Mining Professionals, Brisbane chapter.

You now have the three spotlights, a self-assessment to show you where you stand and your first practice to take with you tomorrow morning.

Right now, somewhere in your organisation, someone is about to get pulled into an exciting project, invited to speak at an event or recommended for a role that wasn't even on their radar. It's time to make sure that person is you.

Spotlight one

This part is all about you and your relationship with your own work. Before you share your work with others, you need to figure out two things.

Firstly, you need to decide what you want to be known for. You'll do this by taking yourself out for a 60-minute Fame field trip.

Secondly, how do you make sure your work stands out? You'll learn how to cast light on the right parts to ensure your contribution cuts through.

Good work is the baseline

I'm going to make an assumption here: you're good at your job, and you meet or exceed expectations. Is that fair? That must be the baseline before we proceed. Shining the spotlight on your work is pointless if you're not meeting the expectations of your role. If that's the case, start there. Chat to your manager about options for growing your technical capability, so you can do your day job well. Once you've hit the baseline? Let's goooooo!

As you work through this spotlight, your goal is to change how people view your contribution. This is because your contribution spans the entire stage — but only some parts are lit.

People form perceptions from what they see and hear — that's all they have. Research confirms arriving early, for example, shapes positive first impressions. Numerous studies have linked on-time arrivals to perceptions of conscientiousness and agreeableness, boosting likability and workplace ratings, while tardiness signals unreliability.[5] But it's not just what time you start work that matters. Ask a sharp question at a town hall? People peg you as insightful. Share clear updates focused on their needs? You're reliable. These signals broadcast constantly (intentionally or not), and they build your reputation one contribution at a time. Your reputation is just the sum of other people's perceptions of you, built up over hundreds of small moments.

If you leave what gets noticed to chance, the wrong things might stand out, or nothing stands out at all. You could be doing all the things on your stage, and your audience can still walk away with no clear perception of what you do or why it matters.

You control your own 'stage lighting' by choosing what to highlight, how to frame it and who sees it. Get the lighting right here, and everything that follows has a stronger foundation. The skills you learn in this spotlight — including speaking in other people's language, using pattern interrupts to command attention and framing your work around results — are skills that shape perception in every part of your work life.

Contribution is essential, but on its own it is not sufficient. You can do brilliant work and still be overlooked because the people who matter are only seeing a fraction of what you do, and they are forming their perception based on that. Are you shaping the story others see about you, and is it the one you want? If not, you have the power to change it.

This part will guide you through making sure your contribution shines in the right places and with the right people.

Scene 2

What do you want to be famous for?

A lot of smart people become known for whatever lands on their desk most often. They get rewarded for being useful, dependable and good in a crisis, and then wake up one day realising they are famous for the wrong thing. Getting noticed for work you don't actually want is a trap. That is how talented people get typecast. So, before we go any further, you need to answer one question: what do you want to be famous for?

We're going to spend 60 minutes getting clear on the direction that matters most for your Work Fame — via a Work Fame field trip.

The Work Fame field trip

Take yourself somewhere that's not your desk and not your couch — perhaps a cafe with good coffee, a park bench with snacks or a rooftop bar with a view that makes you feel like anything is possible. The reason matters because when you're surrounded by your usual environment, you tend to think your usual thoughts.

Here's what to pack for your Work Fame field trip:

- *An A3 sketchpad:* This is important. Working on a surface bigger than usual somehow gives your thinking permission to expand.
- *Coloured pens:* Different colours help you see patterns and highlight what matters most to you.
- A *laptop or tablet with bigger screen real estate:* Preferably, don't use your phone, because you will glance at notifications.
- *A timer:* Again, try to avoid using your phone. Try the timer on your laptop or tablet.
- *Snacks:* Obviously.

Quick tip: Document the process to make it real. While you take yourself on this field trip, for example, I'd love you to take a photo and post it on socials. Tag me @leannehughes (I'll comment back). I want to see where you're dreaming big!

The following sections outline your field trip itinerary.

The drain/gain audit (20 minutes)

Draw two columns on your sketchpad. On the left, write 'Drain'. On the right, write 'Gain'. Open your calendar and go through it meeting by meeting, project by project, for the last month. For each entry, run a quick gut-check. If it gave you energy, write a short note in the Gain column. If it drained you, write it in the Drain column. If it was neutral, skip it.

Next, do the same with your inbox and sent items from the last few weeks. Which emails did you enjoy receiving? Which would you happily unsubscribe from for life? Pay special attention to your sent items. The emails you wrote quickly and enthusiastically tell you something. The ones you drafted, rewrote and sat on for two days tell you something else.

The key here is using your Drain and Gain columns to increase specificity. 'I love working with people' is too vague to be useful. 'I love helping someone brainstorm their way to a first step they can take that day' is specific enough to act on. I am good at picking up new technology, but it drains my energy telling people where to click on a screen and I don't want to be IT support. So, I write articles sharing my favourite tech stacks instead. The specificity is everything.

Aim for at least six items in each of your Drain and Gain columns.

Sharpen the drain (5 minutes)

Now pause and look at your Drain column properly. This list is giving you useful information. Look for patterns. What do these items have in common? Is it the topic itself that's draining you, or the way the work is happening? Are you tired of reactive work, too much handholding, endless approvals and unclear ownership, or work that feels invisible and hard to talk about?

Circle the three items that drain you most consistently. Then, next to each one, write one word that explains why it drains you. Maybe it's:

- repetitive
- political
- low value
- slow
- unclear
- performative
- lonely
- overly detailed
- disconnected from what you care about.

Your Drain list can help highlight what kind of work, pace, environment and role you want to avoid. Before you move on, ask yourself: what does this list suggest I need less of? You don't need to solve it all now, just notice the themes.

Write your dream list (10 minutes)

Flip the page on your sketchpad and set your timer for ten minutes. For all of those minutes, your pen doesn't leave the paper. Don't judge what comes out. Don't ask 'but how?' Don't cross anything out. We are going for volume here. Simply complete this sentence over and over: 'Wouldn't it be amazing if…'

The ideas you write down can go well beyond your current role, your current company and your current city. At least half of these ideas should feel slightly scary. If your list feels sensible and achievable, you're not dreaming big enough. Push past the realistic stuff.

For example, wouldn't it be amazing if:

- 'I was flown to New York to speak at that conference?'
- 'Someone senior asked me to lead that project?'
- 'I wrote something that got shared by someone I admire?'
- 'My manager told me I was the first person they thought of for this opportunity?'
- 'I got invited onto my favourite podcast?'
- 'I got paid to do the thing I would happily do for free?'
- 'I was paid for three months to conduct research on _____?'
- 'I became the go-to person for ______ in my organisation?'

Those are just starting points. Your list should be wilder, more personal and more specific than mine.

Take a quick break

When the timer for writing your dream list goes off, get up. Walk around. Get a refill. Let your subconscious do some work.

Expect and offer (20 minutes)

This step is about making your dreams a bit more real. Open a new page in your sketchpad and draw two columns: Expect and Offer. The Expect column is for what you want to be true 12 months from now. The Offer column is for what you're willing to do to earn it.

Review your Gain column and your dream list. Pick your top five items and write them under Expect. Next to each one, take a guess at what it might take to get there.

Prompt yourself with questions like the following:

- 'What am I willing to say yes to that I have been avoiding?'
- 'What am I willing to do differently from what I have been doing?'
- 'What new skill must I learn?'
- 'What am I willing to stop doing?'

The following table provides some examples for the Expect and Offer columns.

Example entries for your Expect and Offer columns

Expect	Offer
To be flown somewhere exciting for work	Tell my manager I'm open to exploring overseas options; reach out to my colleagues in the UK and find out what clients are requesting
To do more strategic work	Block time each week for higher-level thinking; start sharing recommendations instead of just updates
To speak at my favourite conference	Reskill on a new methodology; connect with the conference organisers on LinkedIn

If your Offer column feels vague, that is fine. The rest of this book is your toolkit. Come back to this page as you read and fill in the specifics.

Your direction (5 minutes)

Before you pack up, complete this sentence: 'I want to be famous for …' For example:

- 'I want to be famous for making clients feel like they are in ridiculously good hands.'
- 'I want to be famous for turning half-baked ideas into something people can use.'

Make this statement light. This is a first draft. But writing it down, even roughly, turns everything you just did into a direction you can follow. You can sharpen your direction as you work through these pages. Now do these two things:

1. Take a photo of your one sentence and set it as your phone wallpaper for the next week.
2. Set a calendar reminder for seven days from now to review your notes and check if you can add, remove or edit anything.

Give yourself a high five

You have just spent 60 minutes figuring out what you want to be known for. That's your destination. Now you need to check where you're starting from, because a gap might exist between the two.

Scene 3

Rewrite your script

You can't outwork an outdated story. Your manager doesn't see everything you do, and your manager-once-removed sees even less. The executive who decides whether you get the stretch project or the promotion has probably never watched you work at all. They are making decisions based on what they have heard, what they have been told and the handful of interactions they have had with you directly. That is what your reputation is built on — fragments, impressions and incomplete stories.

We all use similar fragments when making judgements. Think about the last time someone asked you what another team in your organisation does. You probably said something generic and slightly wrong — 'Oh, they handle compliance', for example, or 'They do the tech stuff', 'They sort out onboarding, I think?' You never see the full picture, so you fill in the blanks with whatever is top of mind, based on the tiny sliver of work you do see. Once that narrative is set, however, it is remarkably sticky. People don't update their mental model of you unless you give them a reason to.

Social psychology research shows that people make snap judgements about competence from very small behavioural cues. Researchers Nalini Ambady and Robert Rosenthal's work on 'thin slices' found that observers can form surprisingly strong impressions of people from only brief observations.[6] That person who fixed a spreadsheet once, for example, is still 'the Excel person' even though they have moved into strategy.

These narratives run on autopilot, and they are running right now about you whether you like it or not. You might respond to this with frustration (I can totally relate) or try working harder. *'If I just deliver better results, surely people will notice!'* That makes total sense until you realise that more effort doesn't fix a perception problem. You can't outwork an outdated story; you must update it.

Let's see what version of you exists in other people's heads right now.

The meme exercise

You might remember the classic meme from 2012 that compares versions of 'What my friends think I do' with 'What I actually do'. It's funny because it captures the difference between perception and reality — and the version of you that exists in other people's heads can be wildly different from the version that shows up to work every day.

You can do a similar comparison right now on a piece of paper. Keep it to four boxes (not the full six from the original meme) and label them as follows:

- What my manager thinks I do
- What other teams think I do
- What I think I do
- What I actually do.

Fill these boxes in based on where you think the perception of you is today. You can draw images, write random words or use bullet points; it's up to you.

The following table provides some prompts.

Comparing different perceptions of you and your work

What my manager thinks I do	**What other teams think I do**
• If your manager had to describe your value in one sentence at a talent review, what would they say? • What do they come to you for most often? • If they were recommending you for a new role, what story would they share about you?	• If someone from another function was explaining your role to a new starter, what would they say? • When other departments mention you, what do they associate you with? • What is the one request you always get from other departments? • If you left the business tomorrow, what would they miss?
What I think I do	**What I actually do**
• If you were pitching yourself for a stretch project right now, how would you describe what you do and why it matters? • What are you most proud of in the last six months that you have not really talked about? • If you could put one project or contribution on a billboard, which one would it be? • What do you wish people understood about your role?	• If someone sat next to you for a full week, what would surprise them most? • What consumes most of your time that nobody outside your team knows about? • What problems do you quietly solve before anyone else even notices they exist?

What stands out?

You're not looking for one perfect answer here. You're looking for what feels off. Where is the biggest mismatch in perception and understanding?

Each gap tells you something different. For example:

- *Compare what you actually do versus what other teams think you do:* A gap here might indicate that your technical contribution is stronger than your visibility. Your best contribution is staying trapped inside your own team.
- *Compare what you actually do versus what your manager thinks you do:* A gap here might indicate that your value is not translating upwards enough.
- *Compare what you think you do versus what you actually spend your time doing:* A gap here might indicate that you're reinforcing a reputation you don't even want. Your aspirations are great, but your calendar tells a different story.

Verify your assumptions

This exercise gets even more useful when you stop guessing. Pick one person from each group (your manager, someone from another team, and a peer or collaborator) and ask them one question: 'When you think about me at work, what do you think I'm best known for?'

Compare their answers with what you've included in your four boxes. Where were you right? Where were you off? What surprised you?

What if your boxes match?

If your four boxes look roughly the same to the answers provided by outsiders, you still have one question to answer: is this aligned to what you want to be famous for?

If yes, keep going. Just know that reputations need maintenance. The minute your role shifts, a restructure happens or you move teams, people start rewriting the story.

If no, you're typecast. People can describe you clearly, but the description is not where you want to live. The next step is not working harder. It is deliberately changing the scenes people see you in.

Close the gap

You now have two things: a direction from the Work Fame field trip, and a diagnostic from the meme exercise. The distance between them is your visibility gap. Everything that follows in this book is designed to close it.

The next scene starts with the fastest way to close that gap: learning to speak in the language your audience already uses.

Scene 4

Going on tour

It's time to pack your bags, you're going on tour — a listening tour! A listening tour is a deliberate, short-term project where you schedule 20-minute, one-on-one conversations with five to ten people across your business or industry. You're not there to pitch ideas or solve problems. Instead, you just ask a few strategic questions, sit back and listen.

While it might sound like a lot of work, a listening tour is the highest return-on-investment (ROI) activity you can do for your Work Fame. Here are the returns it can provide:

- *For them:* It makes people feel deeply respected, valued and heard — which is incredibly rare in a busy workplace. (Have you ever been invited to be a guest on a listening tour? For me, it's super rare.)
- *For your relationships:* It builds trust and visibility across different teams and levels, expanding your network beyond your immediate silo.
- *For your Work Fame:* It gives you the exact vocabulary your stakeholders use to describe their problems. When you use their words to pitch your future ideas, your contributions feel instantly relevant. You're no longer guessing what they care about; you know for sure.

I've run dozens of listening tours, and they can be quite simple to set up. Here's an example email I sent to my list:

> I would love to know: What's the biggest problem you're facing right now? Let's catch up on my global listening tour! I'd love to chat with you over a Zoom call.

Over the next month, 20 people booked 25-minute calls. I arrived at each conversation with a few questions, stayed quiet most of the time, and learned more than I had in months of guessing. The process was energising, got me out of my own head and gave me a wealth of new ideas.

When I later launched a new service, the people who'd been on my listening tour were the first to sign up. I hadn't planned that and didn't go on tour with the intention of selling to anyone; however, by including them in my process, I'd built genuine investment in what I was creating.

When people contribute to your thinking, they become champions of the outcome.

Learn the local language

The listening tour gave me a second, unexpected gift: the exact words my audience used to describe their problems.

When I launched a digital program, I wrote the sales page with this line:

> This program is for solopreneurs who want to grow their client list and book more workshops, without being at the mercy of social media.

One of the first participants to sign up, Maria, had been on the listening tour. She wrote to tell me, 'YES! This speaks exactly to what

I am hoping to explore'. The irony is that Maria had shared that exact phrase with me on the listening tour. I simply played her own words right back to her.

In a Dutch field study, waitresses who repeated customers' orders back word for word received significantly larger tips than those who responded with equally warm but different phrases like, 'Coming right up!'[7] The difference had nothing to do with friendliness. What mattered was mirroring the customer's exact language, which sent a simple signal: 'I heard you, and I understood you'.

I started using this everywhere. I'd spot questions in my online forum and create podcast episodes with the exact same title as their question. People started messaging me with questions like, 'How do you get inside my brain?' I wasn't a mind-reader; I was simply learning the local language.

When you use the exact phrases your stakeholders, leaders and colleagues use to describe their challenges, your contributions feel instantly relevant. You're speaking their language.

What happens when you listen

I recently worked with an Asia–Pacific recruitment team who felt invisible. They wanted to build their internal brand and earn a seat at the table, so I challenged them to go on a listening tour. When we met two weeks later, the results were striking:

- One team member told me, 'The three managers I spoke to said this was the first time someone had reached out just to ask for their opinion'.
- Another found that giving people space to talk completely changed their strategy: 'I suddenly realised we needed to

shift our approach'. One senior consultant emailed the team member afterwards saying, 'It was so nice to chat. I feel like I've been heard'.

- A third admitted the tour exposed their blind spots: 'Our colleagues questioned current approaches we hadn't even considered. It seems obvious now, but honestly? We hadn't thought of it'.

Through conversation alone, this team achieved a massive ROI in just 14 days. They made their work better by learning what they'd missed, they built deep goodwill with people who felt valued, and they put themselves on the radar of leaders who now saw them as strategic partners.

Your listening tour instructions

Ready to try this? Here's a step-by-step guide.

Choose your people

Make a list of five to ten people whose perspective you value and who you'd like to build a stronger relationship with. Think across levels, functions and teams. The best listening tour guests are the ones who see things from a different perspective to you.

Invite them

Reach out with a simple, genuine message. A phone call or in-person ask is ideal, but email works too. Here's a template you can adapt:

> Subject: *[name]*, I'd love your perspective
>
> Hi *[name]*,
>
> I'm working on *[project/initiative]*, and I admire your perspective on *[relevant area]*. I'm doing a short listening

> tour to hear from people across the business, and I was wondering if you'd have 20 minutes for a conversation?
>
> I looked at your calendar and can offer these times: *[option A]* or *[option B]*. Alternatively, let me know what works for you.

Listen more than you talk

If you're meeting virtually, record the call (with permission) so you can review the transcript later. If you meet in person, jot down key phrases as you hear them.

Some questions to guide the conversation:

- When you hear *[this initiative/topic]*, what does that mean to you?
- What are you hearing from colleagues about this?
- What are your biggest frustrations in this area?
- If you could wave a magic wand and this was a stunning success, what would that look like?
- Why is this important to you?

The only rule: avoid offering solutions, excuses or stories. Your goal is simply to listen.

Quick tip: While you're there, here's a 'ringer, pinger or dinger' bonus question. Ask, 'How do you prefer to communicate? Would you prefer if I give you a ring (phone call), a ping (message on company apps) or ding (SMS)?' This gets a laugh and is memorable, and you get to know how they prefer you to contact them, which means your messages land in their preferred channel.

Here's what you want to pick up on your tour:

- *Their exact phrases:* Write down what people say, not your summary of it. When someone tells you, 'We are drowning in approval processes' and you later walk into a meeting and say, 'I know the approval processes have been a real pain point', they feel heard. Compare that with, 'I understand there are some process challenges'. This is in the same theme but has a completely different impact. The specificity is what makes it land.

- *The things they only say one-on-one:* This is where the tour earns its real value. In a meeting, people speak carefully. In a one-on-one with no agenda, they usually speak quite frankly.

Review the call transcript or your notes, pull out verbatim phrases that were used and paste them directly into a spreadsheet. Remember — don't change the language they used; that's the most important part! Your spreadsheet can look pretty simple, similar to the example provided in the following table.

Example notes from a listening tour

Name	Excited about	Challenges	Contact Method	Note to self
Raj, Construction Manager	'I love getting a job moving.' 'Nothing beats a site that's running well.' 'Good people make or break a project.'	'Stuff gets dumped on us too late. By the time it gets to site, we're the ones copping it.' 'People in the office don't realise one small delay turns into three.'	Ring (if he doesn't answer send him a text) 'I'm not sitting there watching Outlook all day.'	Very operational. Values speed, and straight talk. Feels friction from head office. Loves Bruno Mars.

Close the loop

Once you've identified broad themes, share a summary back with your tour guests. Let them know what you identified, what the next steps are or how you can help them with their goals (if relevant), and thank them for their time.

Work Fame in action

Megan Bickle

Megan Bickle has spent her career in talent and culture roles across many industries, from video games to tech to fashion. At the time of writing, she's at Rothy's, where she works alongside people who design colour palettes for shoes and handbags. Her instinct with every new industry role is to lead with curiosity and ask questions, such as, 'How did you get into that?' and 'What are the skills and experiences that led you here?' As she told me, 'When I show up and really get to know people as humans, they start to invite me in'.

(continued)

That approach was tested early. When Megan joined a company in the video game industry, one team had a reputation for keeping HR at arm's length. She reached out to one of the leaders on that team and asked, 'Can we go out to coffee sometime? I really want to better understand what you do, because it will better help me in my job'.

That one coffee turned into recurring breakfasts, and those breakfasts led to invitations to team meetings. Over time, the same people who had once been wary of HR started asking Megan for advice—for example, 'How do I give this person feedback?', 'How should I handle this conversation?' and 'Can I run something by you?'

Megan didn't try to force her way in by proving her value up front. She started by showing genuine curiosity and trying to understand how they worked, what mattered to them and what frustrations they were carrying.

Megan put the reasoning behind this perfectly: 'It's so transactional, otherwise; most people only jump on a call to sort the work out and very few take the time to ask, "What do you actually do? What matters to you? What is your world like over here?"'

So often, we reach out to discuss the things we need to get done. But if you step back and ask some good questions, you can understand someone else's world and what they care about. That helps improve your daily interactions with them, and also helps you contribute better.

By the end of your listening tour, you'll have a secret weapon: the exact vocabulary, frustrations and priorities of the people who matter most to your career.

So far, you've done the listening and learned the local language. Now, it's time to speak it. In the next scene, we'll look at exactly how to take those words and turn them into your greatest professional advantage.

Scene 5

Learning your lines

In the last scene, you learned how to listen. In this scene, you're going to learn how to speak. Your goal here is simple: take the vocabulary you gathered on your listening tour and use it to improve how you're perceived at work.

We're going to cover three ideas on how to do this:

1. talk in results
2. get to the point
3. use launch questions.

Talk in results

Let's say you're in a meeting and someone asks for a project update. Most people's natural response is to share what they've been working on, listing the meetings they've attended, spreadsheets built, the hours the team put in, and the hurdles overcome.

When you do this, however, you're talking in 'task' language. It's a subtle way of saying, 'Look how hard I am working', and sorry, I'll be blunt here, but no-one actually cares what you do. They care about what you create — your results and impact.

When you shift from talking in tasks to talking in results, you speak directly to the things your stakeholders care about—aspects such as time saved, risk reduced, money made or friction removed.

In the following table, I've shared some examples of how you can shift your language in practice. The left column shows example task language (to avoid), while the right column shows the type of language you can use when talking about results and impact. As you can see, everything in the right column is framed around your stakeholder's problem, metrics and opportunities.

Task language versus results language

Task language (about you)	**Results language (about them)**
'We have been working really hard on this project.'	'This project will reduce the approval time from three weeks to five days.'
'The team has put in a lot of hours.'	'The approach we are recommending has been tested at two similar organisations and reduced attrition by 15 per cent.'
'I have been researching best practice approaches.'	'Based on what I have been hearing from the team, the biggest risk right now is *x*, and here is what we are doing about it.'

You're not doing more work—you're just presenting the same work through the lens of what matters to your stakeholders.

Get to the point

In a busy workplace, brevity is the ultimate status move. When you communicate concisely, you signal to everyone in the room that you are confident in your ideas and respectful of their time.

My friend, voice coach Sally Prosser, and I have hosted many 'Get to the point' workshops over the years, largely because getting to the point is incredibly difficult. Early in my career, I thought that more words = more value. What a mistake! Explaining every detail and showcasing all of your efforts doesn't make you look more knowledgeable, in fact, it's the opposite.

A 2025 study from Gartner found almost 40 per cent of managers feel overwhelmed by excessive communication, and that this kind of overload lowers engagement and alignment with corporate strategy, and reduces people's desire to stay with the company.[8]

Waffling can sometimes be associated with a confidence problem. You might feel the need to justify your airtime, prove your worth or walk people through every step so they can see how hard you worked. Sometimes you buy time because you are unsure of your point, and other times you know the point but feel nervous about owning it. However, when you take too long to land your point, your audience stops listening and starts wondering where the conversation is going. In a world of back-to-back meetings and fractured attention spans, brevity is a gift. Renowned consultant and author Alan Weiss summarises this more powerful approach perfectly: 'Tell them everything they need to know, not everything that you know'.

These days, I always prefer a conversation over a presentation. I use a simple five-minute rule: I never talk for longer than five minutes without stopping to check in or ask a question. My goal is to find out what people need, answer what matters and keep the update useful.

When you use a similar approach, you can stay responsive in the moment. You can read the room, notice when people are tapping out and adjust your delivery, instead of bulldozing through a 20-minute monologue just because your slide deck says so.

The US military even has a doctrine for this: BLUF, or bottom line up front. Military briefings are required to start with the most critical piece of information: the decision that needs to be made or the action that needs to be taken. When you use BLUF, you put your recommendation, request or core result in your very first sentence. If your audience or stakeholders need the context, backstory or data, you can then expand to provide it.

Use launch questions

A common communication trap people often fall into is assuming everyone in the room needs the same level of detail. Starting with a launch question instead prevents you from guessing by asking your stakeholders exactly what they need before you start talking. Use these questions at the start of briefing meetings, especially if you are unsure how much context the group has or needs. For example:

- 'How much context do you have on this already?'
- 'Would you prefer the headline or the full picture?'
- 'What are you hoping to get out of this update?'
- 'What specific aspects of this project are you most interested in?'
- 'On a scale from 1 to 10, how would you rate your understanding of this topic?'

Using a launch question allows you to stay flexible and adapt your approach rather than rigidly following your original plan. It also helps ensure your message lands exactly where it needs to.

Scene 6

Every day is an audition

Imagine someone followed you through a week of work, watching your meetings, reading your emails and seeing how you showed up in virtual calls. Based entirely on what they observed, what role would they cast you in?

Work Fame is built in the hundreds of small moments that already exist in your day. Every meeting, every email and every call is an opportunity to shape how people see you.

Your calendar is already a stage

The number one reason I hear for not building Work Fame is time. Yep, I get it, you're already stretched, your calendar is full and the idea of adding anything else feels impossible. The good news is your auditions are already scheduled. You just need to show up to the time slots you already have, with more intention:

- *Already in meetings?* That's an audition for how people see your thinking. Don't just listen and leave. Ask a follow-up question, offer to summarise the actions at the end, volunteer to present an update or host a segment.
- *Already on calls?* That's an audition for how people experience your presence. Rule #1: turn your camera on. I've hosted virtual sessions with hundreds of people signed in, and I can usually count the active cameras on two hands. The moment you switch yours on, you're in a room of 10, not a room of 300. Participate in the chat, react to what others say, share an emoji, come off mute to answer questions and get involved.
- *Already at work?* That's an audition for building relationships. Go to the office. I know I sound like an elder millennial, but being physically present around other people makes a massive difference. If your team isn't in the office, that's even better. It's the perfect time to build relationships with colleagues outside of your department or function.
- *Already drinking coffee?* That's an audition for curiosity and connection. Play coffee roulette: invite someone from a

different team for a coffee every couple of weeks. If the invite feels awkward, try this: 'I've made it a regular habit to get outside of my own team and find out what's happening across the business. I'd love to hear what your world looks like right now'.
- *Already at the offsite?* That's an audition for leadership. When someone asks for a volunteer to host the table discussion, run the energiser or scribe the brainstorm notes, put your hand up.

Every single move in the preceding list happens inside time you're already spending. Not one of these ideas requires staying late.

Before you even say a word

Actors know that casting decisions often start before the first line is spoken, and the same thing happens at work. Beyond what you say and do, people are forming impressions from the signals you send before you have even opened your mouth. These signals are either working for you or against you, in every interaction.

One of the strongest signals you send is your relationship with time. I have another five-minute rule: if someone is more than five minutes late to a call with no message, I leave and suggest we reschedule. When you are consistently on time, you tell people you are reliable, prepared and respectful. If circumstances mean you cannot arrive on time, that's okay! Just send your guest a heads-up to let them know.

When you do show up in person, how you carry yourself matters. When you walk into a room, consider what that entrance says. Are your shoulders back, head up and eyes open to the space around you? Or are you folded over your phone, rushing in and giving off a quiet signal that says, 'Don't talk to me'? Do you smile and look approachable, or do you unintentionally create distance before the conversation has even begun? (For more on this, compare the Walk of Tame with the Walk of Fame, back in scene 1.)

Your wardrobe plays a surprisingly powerful role here, too. A University of Hertfordshire study found that even minor changes in a man's suit changed how confident and successful he appeared in just a few seconds.[9] Participants saw rapid-fire images of the same man in nearly identical suits, with his face cropped out, and then judged how confident, successful and trustworthy he seemed. The tiny tweak of wearing a sharper, tailor-made suit versus a store-bought one, was enough to significantly change their ratings. Participants formed strong opinions within seconds based purely on subtle differences in clothing.

When I moved back to Brisbane to start a new role, one of the first things I did was book a personal stylist. I highly recommend it. Finding clothes that suit me, figuring out what colours work and building a wardrobe that covers different occasions is not my strength, and I was never going to enjoy doing it on my own. In three hours, we put together a full range of outfits for different situations — versatile pieces that I could easily mix and match. The amount of wear I have got out of those clothes has been incredible compared to anything I could have picked up in fast-fashion stores.

Set up your home office

In a hybrid or remote world, your virtual setup is your office — and your stage.

Here's what I prioritise, in order of importance:

- *A good microphone:* This is the single thing that makes the biggest difference. If people cannot hear you clearly, they will stop listening. It doesn't matter how brilliant your point is if static, echo or that hollow laptop-speaker sound are competing with your voice. When I travel anywhere, the microphone comes before the webcam every time. Being heard clearly is more important than being seen in high definition.

- *Camera at eye level:* Position your camera so it feels like a natural conversation. When you're talking, look into the camera rather than at the person on screen to create actual eye contact for the person on the other end.
- *Hands in frame:* Hand gestures are a surprisingly big part of how people read your energy on screen and signalling trust, so keep your hands visible in your camera frame.
- *Lighting:* Face a window or put a lamp behind your screen. If your face is in shadow, people are working harder to read you.
- *A deliberate background:* If possible, choose a real background over a virtual one. Virtual backgrounds can distort your arms and hands, and they often look blurry. A real background lets people get to know you without you having to do much at all. Including your favourite books on a shelf, a poster or a prop that hints at a hobby are all small signals that can start conversations you didn't have to initiate. My background has a green-painted wall that's on-brand, my favourite books and a Moo Deng stuffed toy.

One more thing: in a digital world, first impressions happen before a meeting even starts. On Teams, Zoom and LinkedIn, your profile photo introduces you before you do. Use the same clear, recent photo across every platform. A friend with a decent phone camera and some natural light will get you 90 per cent of the way there.

While things such as a blurry profile photo, a late arrival or a camera that stays off may feel insignificant in the moment, they do add up. People are always forming an impression of you, whether you are actively managing it or not.

Scene 7

Giving your work a better entrance

This scene is about how you deliver your ideas. If you want people to pay attention to your contribution, you need to give it a better entrance. In the following sections, I run through three ideas on how you can communicate with cut-through:

1. *Pattern interrupts:* Breaking the default rules of your office.
2. *New formats:* Swapping long emails for short videos and voice notes.
3. *Owning the objection:* Saying the quiet part out loud before anyone else does.

Pattern interrupts

When the brain sees something it has seen 100 times before, it goes onto autopilot and stops paying attention. A pattern interrupt is a small, intentional break from that default. It is a technique used in sales, psychology and comedy to snap the brain out of autopilot by delivering information in a format the audience was not expecting.

Pattern interrupts do not need to be dramatic, loud or gimmicky; instead, they can look like this:

- sending a one-page visual summary instead of a ten-paragraph email
- recording a 60-second walkthrough video attached to your project update
- scheduling a meeting for 25 minutes instead of the default 30 minutes
- suggesting a walk-and-talk meet-up, instead of another meeting room sit-down.

The test for a good pattern interrupt is simple: does doing something slightly differently make it easier for the other person to understand, decide or act? If the answer is yes, give it a go.

Let me give you an example of a pattern interrupt in action. Years ago, my friend Camilla and I both applied for the same role at a campervan travel company. Over 500 people applied but, somehow, both of us made the shortlist. Her job interview was on Tuesday, and mine was on Wednesday.

The default move for a job interview is to prepare well, dress nicely and answer the questions confidently. But we knew if we both just did that, we'd miss an opportunity to really stand out. Instead, we put our heads together and filmed a two-part documentary series on the campervan company. We found a van from a local backpacker hostel, borrowed it, and shot footage around town. Camilla played volume one in her interview. I showed up the next day with volume two.

John, the founder, hired both of us for a job that was supposed to be for one person. Because of that video content, he created a role where we travelled around Australia and New Zealand filming road trip videos.

The documentary took extra effort, but it changed the trajectory of both our careers.

The assumption flip

Pattern interrupts start by questioning the assumptions baked into the default approach. The following two-minute exercise helps you find yours, and it works for anything: a job application, project update, presentation or meeting.

Draw three columns. In the first column, write down the assumption behind how this is normally done. In the second column, flip that assumption. In the third column, identify one concrete thing you could try.

The following table provides some examples of how to map out a pattern interrupt for a job application.

Crafting a pattern interrupt for a job application

Pattern	Pattern interrupt	One thing to try
A job application includes a CV and a cover letter.	A job application can include multimedia.	Send your CV plus a 60-second video sharing what you'd do in the first 30 days in the job.
I should sound formal and polished to be taken seriously.	I should sound clear, human and decisive.	Open your cover letter with a one-sentence headline covering the problem you'll solve and how you'll do it.
I should wait for them to contact me.	I can reach out first.	After applying, send a connection request and share your intent on LinkedIn.

Choose your format

At work, we tend to reach for the same communication tools every day—emails, Teams calls, meetings and pings. If you want your message to land differently, start by delivering it differently.

Here are two formats that interrupt the default email format.

Short videos

A walkthrough video is a screen recording where the viewer can see your document or screen, hear your voice explaining it and, ideally, see your face in the corner of the screen, as you walk them through a piece of work in real time, just as you would if you were sitting next to them. Tools such as Loom or Canva make this incredibly easy to do.

Videos work really well because text often strips out tone, warmth, intent and energy. An email full of edits and feedback can feel blunt or confusing, even when that was never the intention. A short video solves this and feels more human and useful, and is much harder to misread.

It's also significantly faster. A good walkthrough video can collapse what would have been a 30-minute meeting or a 12-email thread into something someone can watch in three minutes and reply to with a single message.

I've used this format for years. In my 'Get Roasted by Leanne' reviews, clients send me websites, proposals or workshop run sheets. I pull the document up on screen, hit Record and talk through it—highlighting sections, circling key areas, and explaining what I would change and why.

Because a walkthrough video is asynchronous, it also gives people flexibility. They can watch it when it suits them, pause it, replay key parts and respond without needing another meeting in the calendar.

Many tools even let people comment directly underneath, which keeps the conversation moving without dragging everyone onto a call.

This approach is backed by social presence theory, which outlines how different media, such as video feedback, contain more social cues than text, which significantly reduces the psychological distance between you and your colleagues.[10] By letting people see your face and hear your tone, you build trust and prevent the negativity bias that so often plagues written communication.

I use short videos for all sorts of things: giving feedback, talking through proposal options, sending pre-work before a workshop, sharing instructions and following up with key takeaways.

Quick tip: Before you default to another email, ask yourself, 'Would this be easier to explain if I just showed them?'

Voice notes

Voice notes are exactly what they sound like: short, recorded audio messages sent in place of a text or email. They work best when you want your tone to come through clearly or when a written message might seem too cold.

Warning: Not everyone likes voice notes. Some people love them; others genuinely hate them (truly!). Use your judgement, pay attention to the situation and think about your audience. The first time you try one with a new colleague, check in to see whether they prefer them.

The biggest advantage of a voice note is that it lets your energy and intent shine through. For example, a short email asking, 'Can we chat about the project time line?' could sound friendly, urgent or tense, depending entirely on the mood of the person reading it. A voice note removes the guesswork.

I learned this on a 20-week project during COVID. I couldn't travel to the site from Brisbane, so everything had to happen remotely, and

I could not reach one of the maintenance managers. I couldn't get time on his calendar, or on the phone, and the usual email back-and-forth was going nowhere. One day, I sent him a 60-second voice note with a quick question about the project. He replied straightaway, saying, 'I love this'. From then on, that's how we communicated.

The reason that maintenance manager loved the voice note comes down to biology. Recent studies on digital intimacy have found that hearing a human voice creates 'emotional resonance' and a sense of authenticity that text simply can't touch.[11] Voice notes act as a 'relational bridge', giving you the warmth of a real conversation with the flexibility of a text message.

Voice notes are helpful when someone is busy, time zones don't line up or you want to add a personal touch. They keep things conversational without long emails. I use voice notes a lot in my work because they save time, help avoid misunderstandings and make communication feel more human. In my coaching program, Leanne on Demand, clients send me voice notes whenever they want. What I've noticed is that we often answer our own questions just by saying them out loud. It helps us make sense of the challenge.

Quick tip: If you're trying a new format and it feels awkward, using one of these lines can help take the edge off:

- 'Sending a quick video so we don't burn six emails going back and forth.'
- 'I thought I'd share my feedback this way so you can understand the intent.'

Both phrases imply that you chose this format for their benefit, not yours.

Work Fame in action

Andrew Tarvin

Andrew Tarvin is a keynote speaker and globally recognised expert on humour in the workplace. But he started his career as a project manager at Procter & Gamble, where he discovered something important: being efficient is not the same as being effective. Yes, he could throw together a deck quickly. Yes, he could run the meeting and get through the content. However, like a lot of workplace communication, his content was in danger of becoming technically correct and instantly forgettable. So, he started experimenting.

After reading that Alfred Hitchcock used to sneak himself into his own films, even if it was just a silhouette in the background, Andrew decided to do his own version of this in PowerPoint. He began hiding an image of himself in every presentation.

Sometimes it was obvious, sometimes tucked away. One time he even 'drew' a picture of himself using the cells of an Excel sheet. Over time, people started to notice the pattern, and it became a little game. Where is AndreWaldo?

(*continued*)

That tiny change made people pay attention.

Andrew also started using more images, more humour and more human moments in his meetings, and people started looking forward to his presentations. They even borrowed some of his ideas for their own.

What's your version of the pattern interrupt?

Own the objection

A powerful way to give your work a better entrance is to name the tension in the room before anyone else does.

When you stand up to present an idea, propose a change or deliver an update, your audience usually has a silent objection running in the background. It might be about budget, timing or even you. When you say the thing everyone is thinking, that objection loses its power. The room relaxes because you have shown that you understand their world, and you're acknowledging the reality honestly instead of pretending it doesn't exist.

I learned this in Mumbai, while running a leadership workshop for a group of construction workers. Arms were crossed and eye contact was minimal. The vibe was unmistakable: 'Who is this person from our Brisbane head office, and what could she possibly teach us about leadership?'

So, I said this out loud and felt the tension wash away—a few people laughed (phew!) and some nodded. It was disarmingly effective and got their attention.

Precision is everything

If you have run a listening tour, you already know what people are worried about, what language they use when they are frustrated and what sits in the background of every conversation. The difference between owning an objection well and doing so clumsily is precision. Saying, 'I know change is hard' is generic and sounds patronising. Saying, 'I know you have been through three system changes in the last 18 months and the last thing you need is another one' is specific and sounds like you have been paying attention.

Think about the next time you will be presenting to a group that might push back. Write down the one thing they are most likely to be thinking but would never say to your face. Then write a single opening sentence that names it directly, and practise saying it out loud.

Delivery is part of the work. A good idea that arrives in a way people didn't expect, in a format that makes it easy to understand and with an opening that shows you have been paying attention gets talked about.

Scene 8

Save the reviews

My accountant hates me. Every tax season I show up with a shoebox of crumpled receipts, half of them faded and a few definitely missing. But work receipts? I'm excellent at those. I keep every screenshot of praise, every recognition email, and every testimonial. To do so, I have a simple system that takes me ten minutes a week, and by the end of this scene, you'll have one too.

The result is a folder you can pull from at a moment's notice, whether you need it for a performance review, a pitch, a job application or just a rough Wednesday when you need reminding that you are a capable human who's good at what they do.

This evidence is yours to create — you're the only one who knows the full picture of what you have done and why it matters. The best time to save a receipt is the moment it appears. The next best time is when you put it in your calendar to do so (ideally, on a weekly basis).

Your work receipts folders

Set up a receipts folder in your inbox and on your desktop. Call it whatever feels right for you — 'Receipts', 'Reviews', 'My Brag File'. What matters is that you have a certain folder where you drop your work receipts as they happen.

The folder is a dumping ground for anything that captures your work at its best. The curation comes later, when you need to pull from your folder. For now, the only rule is when something good happens, save it immediately. Don't tell yourself you will come back to it (you won't!).

Here's what you can start collecting:

- *Five-star reviews:* When someone emails you or sends you a message that says something like, 'That presentation was brilliant', 'Thanks for saving us on that deadline' or 'I have been telling everyone about what your team did', screenshot it. These messages are the most perishable form of proof you have and tend to disappear into chat history within days.
- *Results:* When a project you worked on delivers a measurable result, capture the number — for example, 'Reduced onboarding time from six weeks to three', 'Increased survey response rate from 40 per cent to 78 per cent' or 'Delivered $120K in savings through the new procurement process'. Numbers are the language that senior leaders trust.

- *Testimonials:* If someone gives you positive feedback in a conversation, ask if you can quote them. Say something like, 'Would you mind if I used that in my development review?' and then write it down.
- *Your own one-liners:* At the end of a significant project, take five minutes and write down a quick summary, covering what the problem was, what you did, the result and what you learned.

How to use your work receipts

You can use your work receipts for so many things, including performance reviews, updating your manager in your catch-ups, future job applications and your LinkedIn profile. Probably the most underrated use, however, is looking at them when you're not feeling your best. Maybe you're low on confidence and you're being stretched. Getting that hit of energy that shows you're capable, you're delivering and you can do this can be a great boost.

Without receipts, your career is documented by other people. When you save your own reviews, you take control of the narrative.

Over months and years, your work receipts folders become the most complete record of your professional contribution that exists anywhere — and they can travel with you through every role, every company and every chapter of your working life.

Start your folders this week

Create your two receipts folders right now. Then spend 15 minutes doing a backwards sweep and scrolling through the last month of your inbox. Look for any five-star reviews, recognition emails, results or feedback worth saving. Also check any other correspondence and save any personal one-liners in your desktop folder.

Scene 9

Fund your fame

A few years ago, I was working in a learning and development role and I applied to attend a podcasting conference because I thought it would be valuable. I was learning a lot through podcasts at the time and wanted to understand the medium better. My request was denied by my manager because it wasn't directly related to my role.

I could have accepted that and moved on. Instead, I applied for annual leave and paid for my own ticket — and what happened at that conference changed my life. A few months later, I launched my *First Time Facilitator* podcast. That podcast has run for over 250 episodes, introduced me to people I would never have met (including my author heroes!), and become one of the foundations for everything I have built since.

The company said no. I said yes anyway.

This scene is about taking ownership of your own growth, with your money and your time.

Your two development budgets

When you think about investing in your own development, you probably default to thinking about the financial cost of things like conferences, courses and certifications. That matters, but you can work another budget as well—your time budget. You can use this budget to explore the internet, AI, YouTube, free webinars, podcasts and open-source courses. The amount you can learn for zero dollars is staggering, but the cost is your time outside work.

Work Famous people run two development budgets: a financial one and a time one. Both require the same discipline. You set an amount aside and protect it, and then spend this budget on things that move you towards what you want to be known for.

Remembering what you're working towards

Before you spend a cent or an hour, you need to know what gap you're trying to close. Go back to your Work Fame field trip notes and your visibility gap exercise. What role are you moving towards? What skills are you missing? What would make the biggest difference to how you're perceived in the next 12 months?

In the first instance, try to connect your development to something your organisation cares about. If you can frame your request as a win for the business and a win for your growth, your company may fund it. If it falls outside what they consider relevant, don't let that be the end of the conversation. Instead, let it be the beginning of a different one: the one you have with yourself about what you're willing to invest.

Work Fame in action

Sophia Arkinstall

Sophia Arkinstall's career spans health science, government, universities, a startup accelerator in Paris and a decade at a private-sector city development company—and it's a great example of what self-investment looks like. She started to realise that writing reports and being great in meetings was getting her nowhere. 'I was really, really great at research', she told me. 'But that was my brand. The chairman would call me "the researcher" and I didn't want to be that person anymore.'

She was shy, but she knew that if she stayed inside her comfort zone, the perception people had of her when she first walked in the door was never going to shift. So, she started driving her own development, on her own terms.

This began with entering an internal innovation competition about the future of cities. Sophia won the prize—a trip to Melbourne. While she was there, she made a 'smart city' vlog. She then started travelling to cities around the world on her own

(*continued*)

initiative, filming videos about the technology and the people she found there, visiting cities such as Queenstown, London, Paris, Oslo, Tel Aviv and Dubai. The vlogs were partly about building her knowledge, but they were also about pushing past her shyness and developing the confidence to tell a compelling story, something she needed in an industry where people struggle to imagine the future unless you can make it vivid for them.

During her MBA, Sophia took on more technology tours than anyone else in her cohort. She visited Tesla, met with the AI research teams for Meta and Google, spent time at Stanford and attended events in San Francisco.

She asked her company for approval to attend, and they agreed to let her go without taking leave. Most of the time, she was paying her own way. Every time she came back, she presented what she'd learned in the company's lunch and learn sessions. She didn't always feel like she had enough official work projects to justify presenting, but she had something better: insight from the outside world that nobody else in the business had. The chairman and the CEO would attend and listen to everything she'd brought back.

Sophia also made a deliberate decision to go beyond her direct manager. She'd learned that if she only shared her thinking with her immediate team, a filtered version reached leadership. So, she built direct relationships with the CEO and the chairman and shared her learnings with them directly.

All this self-investment and contribution resulted in Sophia being given the smart cities portfolio and leading the transport mobility project—opportunities that wouldn't have come her way had she not demonstrated her curiosity around technology and innovation. She got promoted, and she broke out of the 'researcher' label that had followed her for a decade.

Today, Sophia runs AI & Society, a community that brings people from non-technical backgrounds into the same room as technical people to have informed, human conversations about AI. Launched in Brisbane in January 2025 with just 20 people, the community has grown to over 3000 members across Australia. AI & Society hosts seminars, workshops, roundtables and hands-on AI lab sessions—creating spaces where curiosity is the entry point, not a computer science degree.

Building your development budgets

Here's how to build and protect both your financial and time budgets.

The financial budget

Set aside a percentage of your income for professional growth—saving even 2 to 5 per cent makes a difference. As soon as you're paid, move the amount into a separate account. Top it up with any tax rebates you receive for work-related expenses.

Prioritise experiences that your company would never fund, such as:

- conferences that don't neatly align with your current job description (or are in your favourite city)
- courses that build skills for where you're headed, not where you currently are
- trips that put you in rooms with people outside your usual circle.

The time budget

Block recurring time for self-directed learning and protect it. Use this for free courses, a podcast deep-dive, the AI tool you want to learn, articles you want to write and skills you've been meaning to build. The compounding effect of even two protected hours a week is extraordinary over a year.

Boomerang what you learn

Whatever you invest in, bring the learning back. Doing so, firstly, helps you retain it (because the best way to learn something is to teach someone else) and, secondly, helps build your profile.

For more on this, jump to scene 17 (Hosting a lunch and learn) to discover how to deliver a powerful share-back.

Why investing in yourself builds your Work Fame

When you invest in yourself, you take control of your own trajectory. You're no longer waiting for permission to grow. You're building skills, experiences and stories that your current role never would have given you.

The worst that happens? You learn something new, meet interesting people, have a story to tell and maybe something that you can use to your advantage in future.

The best? It changes the entire trajectory of your career.

Spotlight check: Contribution

Before you move into the next spotlight, stop here for a moment to reflect.

Contribution is where Work Fame begins because it gives everything else something real to stand on. This part of the book is less about working harder, and more about getting clearer on what you want to be known for, spotting the gap between what you do and what other people notice, and making sure your work has enough substance and shape to build a reputation on. Your goal is to make what you already do land more clearly.

Now is a good time to ask yourself honestly: is your Contribution spotlight illuminating your value, or is it flickering?

Rate this spotlight

On a scale of 1 to 10, how lit up is your Contribution spotlight right now? Rate yourself based on the following:

- *1:* I am busy, useful and probably under-recognised, but I am not being intentional about any of it.
- *10:* I know exactly what I want to be known for and my work is landing clearly with the people who matter.

Write your number down. What would it look like if you were one to two points higher? What would you do differently?

Three questions to reflect on

Reflect on the following to work out where to focus your Contribution spotlight:

1. *What do you want to be famous for at work?* What is the one thing you want people to associate with your name—not your job title, but your specific contribution?
2. *What valuable work is still too hidden?* Where are you quietly solving problems, improving things, helping others or creating results that are not being noticed clearly enough?
3. *Where are you staying busy but not becoming memorable?* What could you do less of so you can put more energy into the work that builds the reputation you want?

Spotlight two

This spotlight is all about the relationships in your professional world that open doors, and how you can build these relationships to brighten your Work Fame.

Work Fame does not happen in isolation. Sooner or later, someone will mention your name, pass along an opportunity or remember you at exactly the right moment. That person is not a random fan; they're usually someone you've built a relationship with, kept in touch with or shown what you can do — through your conversations.

Why conversations?

Promotions, recommendations, introductions and the chance to take on high-visibility work are all opportunities distributed by people through conversations. This spotlight works in two ways:

- *One-to-one:* This is about becoming comfortable having meaningful conversations and genuinely supporting the people you know. You will look at who is already in your network, focus your energy on the right connections, identify people you can learn from and learn how to reach out in a way that feels natural rather than transactional. You will also find your 'friendtors' — and discover how to stay in people's minds between catch-ups.
- *One-to-many:* Here, you become the host. You bring people together, shape the conversation and share your experience in a space you have created, whether that's a lunch and learn, a panel, a workshop, or an online community.

Scene 10

People are people (even in the C-suite)

Early in my career, I was called into my first exec meeting to present on people strategy. My boss was in the room, but I knew the material best. My section was scheduled for 11 am. The meeting ran late, and I was not called in until 2 pm. By then I was starving, tired and completely in my own head. When I finally walked in, there wasn't even a seat at the table. I found a spare chair about a metre back and sat there without moving it closer, I was that intimidated.

I let them talk about what was on the screen. I'm horrified to admit that I didn't add anything to the conversation — not one word. I walked out full of regret, knowing I had wasted a great opportunity to make a real first impression.

Psychologists call what happened to me in that room 'power distance belief' — or the degree to which we accept inequality as 'normal'. When we put leaders on a pedestal, we trigger a literal 'fear of authority' that blocks our ability to communicate effectively.[12] That feeling of being an 'intruder' in the room is a psychological barrier that prevents you from sharing the very expertise you were hired for.

Status, titles and influence are real. But when we start treating the org chart as a scoreboard for human value — when we decide that a job title makes someone more worthy than us — we hand over our confidence before the conversation even begins.

Just knock on the door

Donna started at a global company 15 years ago, in the London office. One day, her boss asked her to get a document signed by the CEO.

Donna had come from agency life, where hierarchy wasn't a barrier — you just walked up to people and asked for what you needed. So, she went straight to level six, where the executives sat. A keycard was required for entry and she couldn't get in, so she knocked. The EA opened, Donna explained why she was there, walked into the CEO's office, handed over the document and said, 'Hi, how are you? I'm Donna. I recently started here and just need your signature on this'.

They then had a good chat. He asked about her role and she asked about his day. He signed the document and wished her well, and she headed back to her desk. She thought nothing of it — her boss was, however, shocked. 'What on earth did you do?'

When I asked Donna later, 'If someone had told you in your first week never to go to level six, would you still have done it?' She laughed. 'No! I probably would've sent an email like everyone else.' But that moment stayed with her.

Now, when Donna speaks to teams across the business, she leads with this: 'Whether you're speaking to a CEO or a graduate, it's about how you treat others, how you listen and how you show up. When you approach people with respect and authenticity, they often respond the same way back'.

Drop the hierarchy in your head

The org chart is a reporting structure, not a permission structure. Few organisations have an actual policy that says, 'Don't talk to anyone more than two levels above you'. But often an unspoken culture says exactly that, and it can be a trap if you don't question it. Work Famous people see the org chart differently.

The org chart tells you where someone sits in a decision-making structure. Their title tells you who they report to, what they are accountable for and roughly how much budget they control. What an org chart and a title don't tell you is how approachable someone is, how interested they are in people earlier in their careers or whether they would welcome a good conversation.

The difference between Donna walking up to the CEO's floor and everyone else sending an email is not confidence in the traditional sense; it's having a different set of assumptions.

When you catch yourself thinking, *I couldn't possibly reach out to them*, it's worth asking, *Says who?* A helpful reframe is asking yourself, 'What's the worst realistic outcome if I reach out to that person?' In most cases, the answer is that they don't reply — and your career isn't over. The upside, on the other hand, can be significant.

Quick tip: Keep in mind that anyone more senior than you also has a career backstory. They were once a beginner too, nervous in a meeting or unsure whether they belonged.

Work Fame in action

Ren Anders

Ren Anders was a 'theatre kid' who almost became a lawyer. She was at Duke University, studying political science and checking all the boxes for law school because she felt the societal pressure to do something 'serious'. Then, a random adviser changed her life with one word.

Ren asked the adviser, 'What do you recommend to people who are pre-law but don't want to be lawyers?'

The adviser said, 'Don't.'

That was the end of law school and the start of Ren's career. She applied for the NBC Page Program, a dream she'd had since she was 14. The acceptance rate was less than 1 per cent. She got in.

She was 22 and working at *The Today Show* in New York City. Her boss was the lead booker, a veteran of 15 years who had zero interest in meeting another celebrity. One day, her boss handed her an opportunity: 'Someone has to be there. You're going to go, and you're going to be me'.

Ren had been on the job for weeks. Suddenly, she was the sole representative for the show, walking into green rooms with Kim Kardashian, Olympic athletes and Jimmy Fallon, all of them arriving with full teams and a million questions.

She had a choice: show up terrified or trick her brain. She chose the trick. Every time she walked into a room, she told herself, 'I belong here. I am the lead booker of *The Today Show*'.

It worked for the role—and it rewired how she saw herself permanently. 'If I can be in a room with the most powerful people in the industry, I can be in a room with anyone. No-one is going to scare me or intimidate me.'

She sees what hierarchy does to others and it bothers her. 'It makes me sad when people get nervous and uncomfortable, or talk down to themselves because they feel like they're less than.

(*continued*)

I've always led with the idea that I deserve to be respected as much as anyone else in the room, regardless of how famous or old they are, where they grew up, or what they do.'

Ren walks into every room ready for the opportunity, rather than thinking she shouldn't be there. She asks better questions—such as, 'Why not me? Why can't I lead this campaign? Why can't I host this event? Someone has to do it, so why not me?'

Today, Ren works as the Gen Z Assistant to Cody Rigsby, one of Peloton's most recognisable instructors. She also produces and co-hosts the Tactful Pettiness podcast with Cody and Andrew Chapelle.

Your conversations spotlight can't light up if you set guardrails around who you're allowed to approach. People who build Work Fame talk to people, not titles. Everyone is human, with calendars, pressures, insecurities and, later in their careers, sore backs (or is that just me?).

When you stop treating titles as barriers, conversations become possible, relationships become possible, and the opportunities follow.

Scene 11

Capturing your connections

You already have a network. Every person you've met through a job, project, sporting team, dog park, class, event or random life moment is part of it.

Your relationships are your most underused career asset

A common career mistake is only thinking about your network when you need something like a new job, an introduction or a favour. You reach out, ask and then go quiet again until the next time you need something. I've been the person who does this, and it feels super awkward. I've also been on the receiving end, and that's awkward too.

A landmark longitudinal study published in the *Journal of Applied Psychology* tracked professionals over three consecutive years and found that people who actively built and maintained relationships had higher salaries, faster salary growth and greater career satisfaction than those who didn't, and the effect compounded over time.[13]

In this scene, you're going to do two things. First, you're going to get clear on who is already in your network. Then, you're going to build a simple way to stay on their radar, so your name is top of mind when something neat comes up.

The 20-minute roll call

Set a timer for ten minutes and write down absolutely everyone you know professionally and socially. Don't filter, just write down names as fast as you can.

This list might include:

- current colleagues
- people from your last job and the one before that
- people you went through a graduate program with
- someone you sat next to at a conference
- the person who trained you when you first started
- that colleague who moved to another department and who you keep meaning to catch up with
- sporting friends
- people from your running group, gym or social club
- neighbours, family friends and community contacts
- people you have volunteered with
- former clients, suppliers or collaborators
- online friends you have built a genuine connection with.

When the timer goes off, take a break. Then set it for another ten minutes and scroll through your LinkedIn connections, your email contacts, your phone and your calendar from the last six months. Add anyone you spot who you'd forgotten to your list.

Sort your connections

Open a spreadsheet (or your A3 sketchpad) and set your timer for a final ten minutes. Sort every name from your list into one of three categories: Best, Test and Quest. The following table provides a quick example.

Sorting your connections into Best, Test and Quest

Name	Category
Bob	Test
Nidhi	Quest
Eric	Best

Here are the category definitions.

Best

Your Best group is your priority group. These are the people most likely to open doors for you, back you, recommend you or create opportunities on your behalf. People in this group might include your current manager, a former manager who rated your work highly, a senior leader you worked with on a project, a trusted peer in another function or a former colleague who has moved on but still speaks well of you. Aim for 15 to 20 people in this group.

These are the relationships worth steady, long-term investment. When someone in your Best group hears about an opportunity, your name should be one of the first that comes to mind.

Not all relationships within this group carry the same weight. Some people have far greater influence, reach or decision-making power than others. They might be super-connectors, highly respected in their field or people whose recommendation carries real weight. A strong relationship with even one of these people can change the rooms you get invited into, the people you meet and the shape of your career.

Test

Your Test group has potential. These are people you know a little, used to know or feel genuinely curious about, but the relationship is not strong enough yet to define as Best. Maybe you worked together once, or you met at a conference and got along well.

If you ran into someone in this group tomorrow, you would genuinely want to stop and chat. What makes someone a Test contact is that enough interest, relevance or spark is present to make you think, *There might be something in this.*

A five-year study of 20 million LinkedIn users found that the connections most likely to lead to new opportunities were not close friends or daily colleagues. They were moderately weak ties: people you know but don't speak to constantly.[14] Your Test contacts are, almost by definition, exactly this kind of connection. They sit in the space in between and that, it turns out, is where a lot of career-defining introductions and opportunities start.

The goal with your Test group is to keep these people on your radar and stay open. You might reconnect over something relevant, invite them to an event, send an article that made you think of them or comment on their work.

Some Test contacts will move into your Best group over time. Some will stay in Test or drop off your list entirely. That's fine; this is the real world and not every relationship needs to become a deep or strategic one.

Quest

In your Quest group are people you haven't met yet but genuinely want to connect with and get to know. They might include a senior leader whose career you admire, an industry expert who keeps showing up in rooms you respect, a peer on the rise, or someone in another function who seems to have real influence and credibility.

This is your future-facing list, helping you to spot the people you'd love to have in your world.

Your Quest group also provides the opportunity to have some fun, and I encourage you to dream a bit and think, *Wouldn't it be incredible if my path crossed with...?*

When I started my podcast, I made a dream 100 list of people I would love to interview. One of them was Julian Treasure, whose TED Talk 'How to speak so that people want to listen' had a huge impact on me. He ended up being one of my earliest guests on the show. Sometimes, just having the guts to write down a name, no matter how absurd it might feel in the moment, is the first step.

So, let yourself think bigger here; add the respected expert, the person you admire from afar, a person whose work keeps making you think and, yes, even the A-list celebrities. Don't feel shy—all you're doing is writing these down. You're not sharing this list with anyone else! List the people you would love to know, work with, learn from or just hang out with for a day.

If a name doesn't fit into any of these three categories, leave it on the list uncategorised.

Quick tip: Map the influence of your connections. Some of the most valuable relationships in any organisation are with people whose influence is easy to underestimate. Executive assistants are a perfect example here. They are often close to the most senior leaders in the business, with visibility across priorities, personalities and pressure points that few others have.

Focus your energy

Unfortunately, you don't have the time to treat every connection the same. Some relationships need warmth, some need testing and some need patience, as shown in the following table (overleaf).

Requirements of different types of connections

Group	Focus	Rhythm	What this looks like	What to watch out for
Best	Keep trust warm and stay front of mind	Make contact at least once a year, ideally more often due to a real reason	Send a genuine message when they come to mind. Congratulate them on something specific. Share something useful with a reason. Suggest a coffee, walk, or quick catch-up when it feels natural.	Don't let these relationships go cold for years. But don't turn them into robotic 'just checking in' admin either.
Test	Explore the potential	A few natural touchpoints a year	Comment on their posts. React to a job change, event or interesting update. Suggest a low-commitment catch-up such as a 20-minute call or coffee.	Keep it light until you know whether something is real there.
Quest	Prepare well before you approach	Ongoing light awareness	Follow them or subscribe to their newsletter or podcasts. Notice what they care about.	Don't rush to reach out before you have context. When the time comes to reach out*, you will already have done you pre-work.

*For more on the right ways to reach out, see scene 13, later in this spotlight.

Staying relevant between appearances

Building your connection map is step one. Keeping it alive is where the real work begins. The Work Famous stay relevant between appearances.

Sarah Smith works in government in Queensland, leading innovation programs for startups and founders, and she has built an exceptionally strong professional network. Her first piece of advice is disarmingly simple: 'Build your network from day one'.

Sarah doesn't wait until she needs something to reach out. LinkedIn is the first thing she checks every workday morning, using it as a tool to keep up with what people in her network are up to and stay across their world. She also shares that she uses LinkedIn to recognise other people, telling me, 'It takes two seconds to send someone a congratulations message or acknowledge something they've done, but people genuinely appreciate the effort when you reach out, comment or like their work'.

Another strength of Sarah's approach is that she invests in her relationships before a reason exists to cash it in. She keeps conversations going without an agenda. Then, if she ever does need something, the relationship is already warm — but for her, that's the by-product, not the goal.

Sarah's team was recently asked to run a high-profile event for key stakeholders with only a week's notice. They were able to pull it together because they had the relationships to call people who trusted her when she said, 'We need you in the room'.

Sarah is genuinely interested in people, and that interest is what makes the relationships real. Often, she won't lead with the work stuff, but chat about their life instead. 'If someone is telling me about their kids' sport or their divorce, we connect on a completely different level.'

Sarah also advises engaging with the flywheel of attending events, noting that, 'The more you go to things, the more invitations you'll receive', and emphasises the importance of following through on RSVPs. If you accept an invitation, make the effort to attend and avoid being a no-show.

Ways to reconnect

The best time to stay in touch is before you need anything. Here are six ways to do that, which feel natural and take very little time:

1. *Send a specific congratulations:* For example, 'The way you broke down the time line for our non-technical stakeholders was spot on'. Specificity proves you were paying attention.
2. *Share something helpful and include a reason:* Connect the share to something they said or care about, rather than just forwarding random links or articles; for example, 'You have to listen to this podcast — jump in at the 14-minute mark. It relates to what we chatted about last time we caught up'.
3. *Act on your instinct:* When someone pops into your head, message them then. A quick 'thought of you when I saw this' has far more power when you really mean it in the moment.
4. *Make an introduction:* Connecting two good people is a terrific way to create value; however, this does come with a quick warning: always do the double opt-in first. That means checking with both people separately before you connect them. A quick message to each, like: 'I know someone who I think you would really enjoy meeting. She is working on *x*, and I think there is a natural overlap with what you're doing. Would you be open to an intro?' Wait for them to say yes

before you make the connection. An unsolicited introduction puts someone on the spot. You might have meant well, but you just created an obligation. Getting the double opt-in first also means that when the introduction does happen, both people show up genuinely interested because they already said yes.

5. *Comment on their posts:* Reply to their newsletters. Engage with their thinking publicly. This is one of the lowest-effort, highest-impact ways to stay in someone's world, and it simultaneously charges your Coverage spotlight. (This is a particularly good way to engage with people on your Quest list.)
6. *Host a tiny gathering:* Invite three or four interesting people for coffee, drinks or a quick lunch. Keep the invite simple with something like, 'I've been thinking the four of us would have a great chat about what's happening in our worlds right now'.

Remember — when an opportunity comes up, it usually goes to whoever springs to mind. How you stay connected to people determines whether your name comes up.

Scene 12

Finding your friendtors

One type of relationship doesn't get nearly enough attention in career conversations, and it's probably more useful to you right now than a traditional mentor. It's called 'friendtoring', a mash-up of friend and mentor. The term was coined by Jenny Blake in her book, *Pivot: The Only Move That Matters Is Your Next One,* and it describes something most of us do naturally but rarely do intentionally: peer-to-peer learning. In other words, connecting with people at a similar stage, dealing with similar questions and heading in a similar direction.

A lot of career advice points upward, such as, 'Find a mentor', or 'Learn from someone more senior'. And, yes, mentoring can be genuinely useful. I've designed mentoring programs for organisations and participated as both a mentor and mentee. But I've also seen what happens to a lot of formal mentoring relationships after a few months. The energy drops off, business priorities take over and meetings get quietly pushed. I call it 'mentor fade', and it's extremely common.

A subtler problem also exists here. When someone is more senior than you, often some part of you wants to impress them. So, you don't always reveal when you're genuinely stuck and that limits how honest, and how useful, the learning can be.

Friendtors are different. They're trusted peers — people at a similar stage, or just a few steps ahead, who help you think better, see more clearly and stay connected to what's really happening. Because the power dynamic is roughly equal, the conversations tend to be more honest. You can say what you actually think and admit what you don't know, and because they're close to the same challenges you're facing, their perspective is often more immediately useful than advice from someone ten years ahead of you.

For your Work Fame, friendtors do three important things:

1. *They make your work better:* Peers are often more useful than heroes because they are closer to your reality. Instead of, 'Here's how I did it ten years ago', the conversation becomes, 'Here's what I'm trying now', 'This worked better than I expected' or 'I'm stuck on this, what do you reckon?'
2. *They keep you in the loop:* Friendtors are often the first people to send you something useful. 'This sounds like your kind of thing.' 'I saw this job and thought of you.' 'Have you listened to this episode?' 'You should talk to her.'
3. *They are (or can be) more fun to hang out with because you don't need to perform:* Friendtors also matter for a very practical reason — they are usually just easier and more enjoyable to spend time with, and you can be more honest, more relaxed and more yourself. You can say, 'I have no idea what I'm doing here' or 'Can I show you something half-baked?' without feeling like you need to perform.

What friendtoring can look like

One of the best things about friendtoring is that it doesn't need a formal structure. My first friendtor set-up was called the Quarter

Life Crisis Club. We'd meet at a cafe on a Saturday morning every other month. That was our ritual. Just three people at a similar stage of life and career, checking in and talking through whatever was on our minds, setting mini goals between our sessions, and cheering each other on and encouraging each other to take risks.

Some of my more recent friendtorships are with people I met online. Keynote speaker Andy Storch and I are friendtoring right now. We're both working on books, and we have an online shared word counter. He's in Barcelona, I'm in Brisbane, and we update the word count so we can see each day how the other person is tracking. When someone hasn't updated their section in a few days, we check in. Having that peer accountability is genuinely motivating when you're working on similar goals.

Steph Clarke in Melbourne is another friendtor. We voice-note each other constantly, updating our ongoing conversation whenever something comes up, and we're both solopreneurs with similar business models. It doesn't have an impact on our time for either of us because we respond when we're ready, and we both send each other funny rants or wins through the week. And a shoutout to Petra Zink and Maike Neuhaus — we take our friendtor meet-ups to rooftops, with champagne and hot chips, and ask each other very difficult questions.

Attributes of a great friendtor

Your list of what you want in a friendtor might be slightly different from mine, but here's what I recommend looking for:

- *Positive attitude:* They are encouraging, generous and solutions-focused.
- *Similar goals:* You don't need the same job, but it helps if you're both heading in a similar direction.

- *Not in direct competition:* Being honest and supportive is easier if the relationship doesn't have any awkward rivalry underneath it.
- *Fun to be around:* You enjoy spending time with them; they're the type of person you'd choose to tag along with at a conference, for example.

Finding your friendtors

You might already have friendtors and not realise it. Think about the people you naturally go to when:

- you want to test an idea
- you need a second opinion
- something interesting happens at work
- you want to share a win
- you need someone to tell you the truth.

If you want to be more intentional about building friendtor relationships, consider the following:

- former colleagues
- people in communities you're already part of, such as online groups, industry networks, course cohorts and events
- people on a similar trajectory in a different context (another industry, role or city); the difference in environment makes it fresh.

You don't need a formal structure to start. Instead, start by setting up a one-off event and then seeing if a mutual need emerges to continue catch-ups. These could be in real time or you keep the conversation going through other formats, such as voice notes or shared accountability docs.

A note for leaders and L&D teams

If you work in learning, leadership or culture, friendtoring is worth paying attention to. While mentoring is great for guidance, experience and perspective, friendtoring is great for mutual support, accountability and connection across the business. It is also far easier to scale, because it is not limited by hierarchy.

Your friendtors today are your referral network tomorrow. Don't underestimate the people on the same journey as you.

Scene 13

How to reach out (the right way)

I overheard a conversation at a cafe recently that made me nearly choke on my avocado and sourdough toast. A careers adviser was talking to a recent graduate and sharing her big networking tip for reaching out to industry experts: ‘Message people on LinkedIn and invite them for coffee. Because who doesn’t want a free coffee?’

I’ll tell you who — me, firstly. I mean, I love coffee. But I already have a full calendar, an inbox with replies owing and a demanding sausage dog. And I’m not unusual; we live in a world where people are ‘busy’ as their default. I’m also not saying don’t reach out. You should. Reaching out to people you admire, want to learn from or hope to work with is a terrific move, and I encourage it. But a vague, generic ask such as, ‘Hey, let’s grab a coffee — my shout!’ wastes everyone’s time, including yours.

This scene is all about reaching out the right way. But, first, let’s have a quick look at why this is important.

Why reaching out matters

The people who get the interesting projects, promotions, introductions and unexpected opportunities are usually the ones who have built relationships beyond their immediate circle.

That means you will sometimes need to contact people who have no idea who you are, such as an author whose work changed how you think, someone in another department doing work you admire, a speaker, an industry expert, or someone you've only seen from afar in town halls or on LinkedIn.

This often feels uncomfortable, or like you're bothering someone. But what I've learned from being on both sides of this is that, generally, people are genuinely flattered that you reached out. They want to help. It's just hard to say yes when the ask is vague and they're left trying to figure out what you need.

Quick tip: When you message someone who doesn't know you, their most likely first response is to look you up. They'll check your LinkedIn or might even search for you online, trying to answer this question: 'Is this person legit?' This is where your Coverage spotlight (which we dive into in the next part) does the heavy lifting before you even show up.

The anatomy of a great reach-out message

I almost never say yes to messages from strangers requesting to catch up. But this message from Margaux Grasso was different:

> Hello Leanne,
>
> I was researching some information about workshop facilitation when I landed on one of your videos about how you organise your facilitation material for workshops. I loved your idea of doing a 'VideoAsk' before workshops. I recently ran a workshop for the directors of the company I work for, and I really wish I had done that.
>
> This led me to watch a few more of your videos. Being an F1 fan myself, I like how you compared it to moving from point A to point B quickly. Working in digital marketing, I think clear and concise communication is so powerful, and

> not only in marketing but also in life in general. Personally, I am team Daniel too. He got so unlucky hurting his hand soon after his big comeback.
>
> I am a marine biologist and science communicator turned digital marketer for the past eight years, but considering a career change into workshop facilitation. I sometimes run workshops for the company I work for but recently realised it is what I enjoy most about my job. I find it admirable, and really cool, that you have made a successful career out of workshop facilitation and public speaking.
>
> I would love to learn more about your career path, what it takes to become a workshop facilitator and what you find most challenging about it.
>
> I appreciate that you might be very busy, but I was hoping you would be free for a 15-minute Zoom call in the next couple of weeks?
>
> Best wishes,
>
> Margaux Grasso

I made time for Margaux because her message made it easy to say yes. Let's dissect why.

Margaux got four things right:

1. *She did the work:* She found a specific YouTube video, watched more of my content and explained exactly what drew her to reach out. That 'why you' detail matters enormously. She did more than summarise what I'd said. She connected it to her own experience.
2. *She found a personal hook:* She mentioned Daniel Ricciardo. Now, obviously, anyone who mentions Daniel Ricciardo to me is helping their chances. (Remember the scene at the start of this spotlight? People connect with people, not titles.)

3. *She gave me context:* Margaux gave me enough context about herself that I could picture her situation. I understood where she was at and why she was reaching out now. Notice, it wasn't too much context, though. It was just right—the 'Goldilocks context', if you will!
4. *She made a specific ask:* Instead of saying, 'Let's have a coffee' or 'Let's jump on a call', she asked for a 15-minute Zoom call. This is contained and easy to fit into a real day.

Have a look at the people on your Quest list. Can you spot anyone you can try this out on? If you have someone in mind, the following sections run through a few more tips to improve your chances.

Start with a referral if you can

Before you go the cold message route, check whether you have an easier path—because a referral is always a better option. If you have a mutual connection, use the double opt-in approach. Ask your mutual connection first: 'Would you be comfortable introducing me to *[person]*, or would you be happy for me to mention your name when I reach out?'

I suggest doing this for three reasons:

1. It respects your contact's relationship with that person.
2. It protects the recipient from unsolicited name-dropping.
3. It protects you from the awkward situation where you mention someone's name and the recipient checks with them, only to discover they had no idea.

Often, asking first leads to something even better: the person offers to introduce you properly.

But what if you don't have a mutual connection? If they're a stranger, try the next approach.

Use a message template

The following provides a basic structure when you need to message someone cold. You can fill in the blanks and edit this template so it sounds more like you.

> Hi *[name],*
>
> I found your *[article/video/podcast episode/post]* about *[topic]* through *[how you found it].* Your point about *[specific idea]* really resonated because *[how it connected to your own experience, what you tried or what it made you rethink].*
>
> A bit about me: I'm a *[your role]* at *[company/context],* and I'm currently *[what you're navigating or working through].* I'm reaching out because *[why this person specifically and why now].*
>
> *[Pick one of these asks:]*
>
> Would you have 15 minutes for a quick Zoom call in the next couple of weeks?
>
> *[or]*
>
> I have two specific questions about *[topic].* If it's easier, I'm happy to send them here or by email, whatever suits you better.
>
> *[or]*
>
> If you've already written or spoken about this somewhere and I've missed it, I'd be grateful to be pointed in the right direction.
>
> Thanks!

Dos and don'ts when reaching out

Here's a quick reference table (overleaf) sharing lines to avoid versus try when reaching out.

How to reach out to people

Don't do this	Do this instead
Say, 'Can I pick your brain?' or 'Let's grab a coffee!' (to someone you've never met)	Say, 'I have two specific questions about *[topic]*. Would you be open to a 15-minute virtual call, or would you prefer I send them here?'
Copy and paste the same message to 50 people	Send three good, targeted messages. If it could work for anyone, it's not specific enough.
Ask questions they've already answered publicly	Spend time digging into their public ideas (including articles, posts and podcast) first. The effort shows, and you'll probably find half your answers without needing to ask.
Send a wall of text about yourself	Give them the 'Goldilocks context'. Provide enough for them to picture your situation and its relevance to the conversation you'd like to have with them.

Quick tip: If you really want to accelerate relationships with people you admire, start a podcast — or a video series or a newsletter where you interview people. When you have a platform, even a tiny one, you're no longer just asking for someone's time. You're offering them something too: an audience, a conversation and a piece of content they can share. Like this idea? Skip ahead to scene 26, which covers starting your own limited series podcast.

And ... action!

Open your Quest list and choose one person you have been meaning to contact. Spend ten minutes doing your homework, looking at what specifically they've written, said or shared that caught your attention. What genuinely connects with your own work? What is your actual ask? Structure your message, and then click Send. (If you feel a little embarrassed afterwards, email me at hello@leannehughes.com with the subject I DID IT and I will send you some virtual high fives.)

Scene 14

From audience to panellist

Chances are, you've sat in a town hall with a question forming in your head, talked yourself out of it, and left wishing you'd said something. Or perhaps a senior leader visited your team, asked if anyone had questions, and you watched the silence stretch while your hand stayed firmly in your lap. You had the insight, the experience and the perspective — and you kept it to yourself.

This scene is about changing that habit, working through two levels of the same skill:

1. *Raise your hand:* This could be at town halls, all-hands meetings or department briefings — any room where you have a chance to ask a question or contribute a perspective.
2. *Take the hot seat:* This includes sitting on panels, and participating in fireside chats, roundtables or industry events — any room where someone has asked you to be the guest instead of the audience.

Raise your hand

Every organisation has a version of this: a room where leaders share updates and invite questions. Whether it's called a town hall, an all-hands or something else, the scenario is the same: a senior leader speaks, and then pauses to ask, 'Any questions?' The room goes quiet. People look at their shoes or, if on a virtual call, everyone stays on mute. The silence stretches. The host tries again: 'No questions at all?' Someone eventually asks a safe question about the office renovation time line.

Stepping up in these meetings and asking a more insightful question is a direct way to increase your visibility and stand out as a leader. Deciding to instead hold back your thoughtful question is a missed chance to shape leaders' perceptions of you.

I have hosted dozens of these events. I have worked with senior leaders on designing them and I can tell you exactly what they are thinking during that silence: *Please, will someone say something!*

When you raise your hand, you're helping the leaders, not just yourself.

Speaking up shows courage and catches leaders' attention because so few do. You become memorable for asking insightful questions.

How to prepare

You can reduce the risk significantly when asking a question by preparing in advance. A lot of what gets shared at these events is predictable. If you have been reading leadership emails, following the news or paying attention to what is coming down the chain, you can anticipate the key themes.

Before the event, write a couple of questions; you might even want to check them with a peer or your manager. Practise saying them out loud, because a question that reads well on paper can sound completely different when you speak it.

When it is your turn, keep it tight—for example:

> Hi, my name is *[name]*. I work in *[department]*. I am curious about *[your question]*.

Remember my tip back in scene 5 about getting to the point. Trust that your leader will ask a clarifying question if they need more information. Often, the mistake isn't asking the question; it's providing too much context and over-explaining yourself. Ask your question and then hand it over.

Quick tip: A big difference exists between asking a genuine question and asking a self-serving one. A self-serving question is just a statement dressed up as a question. It's someone demonstrating their own knowledge rather than genuinely seeking an answer. Don't be that person. Your colleagues can detect that instantly and sense it as a flex. A genuine question comes from curiosity, your own experience and where you sit within the business.

After the event

If a speaker said something that genuinely provoked your curiosity, approach them afterwards and share your thoughts. In person, this can be as simple as waiting for the small crowd to clear and saying, 'I really liked your point about *[specific thing]*. Can I ask you a brief follow-up?' On a virtual call, send them a message straight after: 'Thanks for today. Your point about *[specific thing]* really resonated'.

People rarely do this, and it's memorable when they do.

Work Fame in action

Cherie Canning

Cherie Canning is the founder and director of Luminate Leadership. Oh, and she once sang on stage with Chris Hemsworth (her absolute favourite actor in the world) in front of 3000 colleagues. As a work perk, it doesn't get much better than that, right?

So, I had to ask her: how on earth did this happen?

She shared that when she was working at Flight Centre and returned from maternity leave, she had a fierce drive to make her time at work count. She voluntarily joined the Flight Centre Foundation, co-founded ‘Parent Wise’ (a program connecting parents on parental leave back into the business) and threw herself into her training role with an intensity that was hard to miss, delivering around 70 sessions in six months (almost six times what the role had historically averaged).

Her peers noticed and, at the end of that financial year, fewer than 12 months after returning from maternity leave, her department voted for her to attend the company’s global annual event in Berlin.

That vote put her in the front row at Mercedes Arena, surrounded by 3000 colleagues, with Hemsworth on stage in front of her, flanked by comedians Michael McIntyre and Jimmy Carr. The event was streaming live to Flight Centre offices worldwide. For Cherie, it was already a dream come true.

But the best part happened when McIntyre finished his set and asked for a volunteer. Before anyone else had lifted their arm, Cherie leapt out of her seat and just started running to the stage. Over the next segment, she sang ‘I Will Survive’ with Hemsworth, and traded banter with two of the world’s best comedians, in front of a global audience. It was, in her words, ‘one of the most amazing moments of my life’.

Cherie didn’t get that moment by accident. It was earned through nine months of consistent contribution (volunteering beyond her role, delivering far more than was expected, building a reputation through service rather than self-promotion). That put her in the front row. And being in that front row is what made it possible for her to be the first one on stage.

That’s what raising your hand, consistently and generously, can do for you.

Now, let's learn what taking participation to the next level looks like.

Join the panel

When you become Work Famous, people want to talk to you and ask you questions, and you might be invited to participate in panels, either at work or at industry events. Jumping into the panellist chair can feel daunting. You might worry about freezing up, losing your words or forgetting key points.

In the following sections, I run through what I have learned from being on both sides of that conversation, and from coaching others for their first time in the hot seat.

Prepare like a performer

I am not suggesting you memorise a script, but becoming comfortable with some of your answers is helpful, and allows you to go 'off-script' with confidence.

Often, panel hosts will send through some prep questions (if not, it's always worth proactively asking for them). I always coach my panellists to nail the first answer (no pressure). This is because your anxiety is almost always highest before you start speaking. Once you have delivered your opening answer and heard yourself sound competent, your nervous system settles. Everything after that gets easier.

For each prep question, write two or three bullet points. These are your anchor points. Rehearse these answers out loud but don't feel you have to sit still while doing so — talk through your answers as you go for a walk, for example. Record yourself and play it back to see how you sound or where you can improve. You'll be able to hear which stories unfold smoothly and which ones need tightening.

Create your own container

One of the simplest things you can do when you're answering a question is to give yourself a structure before you jump in. Use something like the following:

> Thanks for your question. I think there are two key things here we need to address.
>
> Firstly, *[insert your point]*.
>
> And, secondly, *[insert your point]*.

This creates a container. Now your brain knows it needs to deliver two things and the audience knows what to expect. You're no longer free-falling through an open-ended answer, hoping you land somewhere useful.

This works for live conversations, virtual panels, one-on-one meetings and any situation where a question catches you slightly off guard.

Work the room

You don't have to carry the entire conversation on your shoulders. A panel or fireside chat is not a monologue. Instead, it is a conversation, and the best guests know how to bring the room in. Try the following:

- *Arrive early:* Before the event, walk around the room and introduce yourself to a few people. Ask what they are hoping to get from the session. This gives you real-time intelligence about what the room cares about and helps you use their language back to them (hello, listening tour principles). It also means you can spot a familiar face in the audience when you're in the hot seat.

- *Throw it to the audience:* If you're sharing a challenge or a perspective, pause and ask the room, 'Hey, I'm curious — raise your hand if you have handled something similar?' This takes the pressure off you, lifts the energy in the room and gives people a reason to feel involved rather than just watching.

Dealing with nerves

You will be nervous. That's normal and a good sign. It means you care about doing a good job. Neen James, a keynote speaker, once told me something that changed how I think about nerves: 'When you stand in service, you cannot be nervous'.

When you focus on how you sound, how you look and whether you're saying the right thing, your anxiety spirals. That's because the spotlight is pointed inward. When you flip it outward and focus on the people in the room, asking yourself, 'How can I help this group? What do they need to hear? What would make this worth their time?', the nerves settle a little because your focus is on their experience.

The nerves are almost always worst in the five minutes before you speak. Once you start talking, they drop. Knowing this helps, because you can plan for it.

These tips also help in the moment:

- *Take a breath before you answer:* It can seem like an eternity to you, but it looks like thoughtfulness to the audience.
- *Keep your hands in sight:* Hand gestures help people read your energy on screen and in person.
- *Remember that your audience doesn't know what you planned to say:* If you skip a point or go in a different direction, it's okay – don't apologise!

Speaking up at a town hall puts your name and your face in front of senior leaders in a context where very few people are willing to step forward. Sitting in the hot seat at a panel or event does the same thing but, this time, you're the one fielding the questions.

Work Fame in action

Andrew Thomas

Early in Andrew Thomas's career at GSK in Australia, he put his hand up at a town hall and asked a question. Afterwards, his mates pulled him aside. 'Why did you do that? Don't draw attention to yourself.'

Andrew listened for a while. Then he asked himself: did he want to keep being one of the cool kids, or did he want to be their boss in five years?

'Your peers at work don't always have your long-term interests at heart when they are giving you advice', he told me. 'It is not that they are nasty. They just don't want you to draw attention to yourself or to them.'

(*continued*)

So, Andrew decided to ignore his mates' advice. He started taking every shot. He sat in the front row. He asked questions. He challenged ideas. He volunteered for things other people avoided.

One of his mentors gave him advice early on: 'The more lateral moves you make early in your career, the better positioned you are to move vertically later'. He did take this advice. Andrew moved laterally through sales, analytics, marketing, and mergers and acquisitions, building a breadth of experience that would make him harder to say no to later.

Then he hit a ceiling. The next step up in Australia was five years away. He could have waited. Instead, he opened his laptop and started writing messages to people he had never met. He reached out cold to senior leaders across the company's Asia–Pacific office. The message was straightforward: 'Here is my story. I am mobile. I am interested. Can we have a chat?'

Within weeks, he had accepted a role in Malaysia, running a business unit at a scale he would have waited years to reach at home. From there, he moved to Singapore, where he managed portfolios across China, India, Japan and Australia. Then he set his sights on the United States, a market people told him was closed. He approached people anyway. He said he would take any role just to get through the door.

Then came a phone call from a sales VP in the United States, offering him a job he had never applied for and did not know existed. Andrew took up the role as one of 100 sales leaders overseeing 2000 representatives. Nobody knew who he was. So, he did what he had been practising since that first town hall in Australia.

He sat in the front row, asked questions and challenged ideas. He was promoted three times in four years. He didn't apply for any of those jobs.

'I don't think I am of exceptional intellect or talent', he told me. 'But I have taken every shot that has been open to me, or I have created room for a shot where there was not one.'

It all began when Andrew raised his hand and took his first opportunity to stand out.

Today, Andrew is Vice President, General Manager of GSK Australia, and now coaches emerging talent within the business. He gives them the same advice to get involved—write down questions before a town hall meeting and raise your hand to ask one, volunteer to host the table conversation at the off-site, say yes to breakfast with the GM. Leaders notice your efforts.

Every room you are already in is a stage. The shift from audience member to memorable contributor happens in the moment you choose to add something instead of simply watching. This week, start small: choose one meeting, prepare one question, and ask it.

Scene 15

The spotlight belongs to the host

Hosting can be one of the biggest Work Fame accelerators in your career (as it has been in mine). It puts you at the front of the room, and gives you a reason to gather people, shape the conversation and create value in public. It also gives you access to people you would never have met in your normal role.

When you step to the front of the room, others start to see you differently. Sociologists argue this is due to what they call 'status characteristics theory'.[15] The idea is that when people enter a group, they quickly scan for cues about who is competent and who has influence, and they use whatever signals are available to form those judgements, even when those signals have nothing to do with the task at hand.

The person running the meeting, introducing the speakers or standing at the front of the room reads as more authoritative, almost automatically. That's what hosting gives you. Before you've shared a single insight, the room has already placed you in a different category.

Reasons to host

Hosting also builds an incredible range of skills very quickly:

- *It sharpens your communication:* When you're introducing speakers, guiding a discussion or summarising what you have heard, you're practising how to speak clearly in front of groups. Conversations rarely go exactly to plan. Someone says something unexpected, a question comes from the audience, or the technology fails. Hosting forces you to think on your feet.
- *It helps boost your network:* Hosting creates a terrific excuse to speak with speakers, guests and participants before and after the session.
- *It teaches you how to read a room:* You learn when energy is dropping, when a conversation needs redirecting and when someone has something interesting to say. That skill carries into meetings, presentations and leadership roles later in your career.

In short, hosting is a fast track for being seen, and being judged as capable and trusted in front of other people.

Hosting action

Tara Chavan saw the benefits of hosting firsthand. She worked in a technical scientific role in drug safety within the pharmaceutical industry. She was good at her job but mostly known within her own function. Then a side project came up around employee engagement and communication, running alongside her day job, and Tara put her hand up.

At the time, the company's global town halls were fairly passive. Someone would share their slides, talk through a few topics, and everyone else would sit there silently watching. When Tara got involved, she changed the format completely. She turned the town halls into something more like a talk show. She was the host, presenters became guests, and the sessions became more conversational, more interactive and more engaging.

For these online sessions, Tara created a virtual background that looked like a couch. Presenters came on and she interviewed them, with talk going back and forth, like you were watching Graham Norton. She used Mentimeter to get the audience voting and interacting. She put people into breakout rooms with cameras on for smaller sessions. After a while, the presenters started coming up with their own ideas for how to get the audience engaged.

Suddenly, Tara had a reason to speak with people across the business. As she put it, 'I got to know people across our department. When global visitors came through, I'd often get invited to meet up with them because I had that connection that sat outside of typical work. I built personal relationships with people I never would have met otherwise'.

Hosting gave her access she would never have had in her original role. She was invited to leadership meetings, dinners and events that would not normally have been on her radar. She even got to travel to a work conference in Greece. In her words, 'My job title wouldn't have got me there. But because I said yes to hosting, I scored these amazing opportunities'.

When it comes to promotions, you also need leaders outside your lane to recognise what you do. Tara shared the following advice: 'The leadership team have to decide who will get promotions. A lot of times you could work very well, but the other leaders don't know who you are, so it's hard for them to advocate for you'.

Hosting also helped with her confidence. Earlier in her career, Tara felt nervous speaking to the head of manufacturing or even the head of her own department. But after hosting multiple sessions, that fear dropped away. 'Now, I'd be fine if I had to talk to the CEO', she told me. Why? 'Because when you start chatting to people, you realise at the end of the day, they're all people.'

As you move through the remaining scenes in this part, think broadly. Everything you're about to learn can be applied across panels, lunch and learns, training sessions, roundtables, town halls, webinars, off-sites and meetings.

Now, let's get you hosting!

Scene 16

Hosting five-star meetings

Think about what happens when a meeting invite lands in your calendar. You likely first check who's running it. Some names make you think, *I'll be there*. Others make you reach for that Decline button. Which one are you when people receive your meeting invite?

The way you run meetings is a direct indication of how you think, how you lead and how much you respect other people's time. It can be one of the most visible things you do at work, and one of the most under-rated opportunities to build your reputation.

Before you start sending invites, though, pause for a moment. Meetings are expensive. They cost time, focus, energy and goodwill. So, before you call one, it's worth asking two quick questions:

1. *Does this even need to be a meeting?* If you need sign-off from one person, go and have that conversation directly. If you're sharing information that doesn't need discussion, send it through another channel.
2. *What needs to happen by the end?* Do you need a decision? A plan? If you can't answer that clearly, the meeting probably isn't ready yet.

Once you've decided it does need to happen, you can then focus on making sure your meetings get five-star reviews — and people are always keen to accept your invites.

Treating a meeting like a movie

Think of your meeting as being similar to a movie production. As shown in the following table, every great film has certain building blocks, and so does every meeting worth attending.

The building blocks of great movies and great meetings

Great movies have ...	Great meetings have ...
The trailer	A clear title, purpose and pre-reading
The casting	The right people in the room, with a clear reason they've been invited
The runtime	A length that matches the purpose
The direction	A host who guides the conversation, brings people in and keeps the meeting on track
The credits	A follow-up with clear actions and ownership

In the following sections, I outline a host's playbook for each of these elements.

The trailer: What people see before the meeting starts

This is your first impression as a host. Give the meeting a clear, specific title, instead of something general like 'Catch-up' or 'Discussion'. Ensure the title tells people why they should show up.

Next, make sure you state the purpose in the invite. One or two sentences is enough — for example:

- 'We're meeting to make a decision on *x*.'
- 'We need to work through these three issues and leave with a plan.'

Send pre-reading or context beforehand if it helps. Not everyone will read it, but you've given them the option to come prepared, and that signals you take your and their time seriously.

The casting: Who's in the room and why

Most meetings have too many people in them because the organiser is being polite, political or cautious. Good casting is the opposite.

Invite people because you're clear on what they will bring and why they need to be there. If someone is only there to 'stay in the loop', send them the notes afterwards (they will love you for doing this!).

Also — and perhaps counterintuitively — the more people you have in your meeting, the less likely people are to speak up. Group size matters and being selective signals respect. It says, 'I have thought about this, your time matters, and I need your perspective for a reason'.

Quick tip: Want to add bonus points to your Work Fame score? Cast beyond your immediate team. That might mean hosting a cross-functional problem-solving session, a debrief that brings together teams who don't normally talk, or a knowledge-sharing session where someone from another part of the business shares something useful. When you do this, people across the organisation get to see you in action.

The runtime: Respect the clock

The length of your meeting is where trust is built or broken. Start on time. Don't wait for latecomers. Don't wait for the most senior person in the room. Don't collect $200. Just start. What you will find is that next time people are more likely to show up on time because they know you mean it.

End on time too or give people an option to wrap up — for example, 'We're running over. Would you prefer to reschedule the remaining items, or spend another ten minutes finishing this properly?'

Don't default to an hour just because your calendar app suggests it. It's remarkable how many of my 20-minute calls end after 20 minutes. Often, people have back-to-back meetings, so even 40- or 50-minute meetings work well, giving people respite between calls.

Every time you run a meeting that starts sharply and finishes when you said it would, you reinforce the same message: this person respects my time.

The direction: How the room feels is your responsibility

When the conversation drifts during your meeting, bring it back. Say something like, 'That's a great point and I want to come back to it, but let's make sure we get through *x* first'. This can feel rude the first few times you do it, but I implore you: everyone else in that meeting wants you to intervene, and people respect hosts who can keep the room moving towards its purpose.

Good direction also means making space for quieter people. Not everyone will speak up unprompted, but that doesn't mean they have nothing to say. To encourage these people, give everyone a moment to think before asking for responses — for example, 'Take 60 seconds to jot down your thoughts, and then we'll go around'. Another option is to pair people up first. These small structural choices change who contributes and what you hear.

Here are some other transition sentences you can have in your toolkit to help steer the conversation:

- *To bring the conversation back to the key point:* 'The thing I keep coming back to is ...' or 'If we zoom out for a second, the core question is ...'
- *To bridge between what someone said and where you want to go:* 'That connects to something I have been hearing from the team, which is ...' or 'Building on that, the thing I think we are missing is ...'

- *To redirect when things are drifting:* 'I want to make sure we get to *[topic]* before we run out of time. Can I jump in on that?'
- *To acknowledge a point while shifting the frame:* 'I hear that, and I think there is another way to look at it…'
- *To create space for a different perspective:* 'I am curious whether anyone is seeing this differently…'

The credits: What happens after the meeting

What happens after the meeting is where most hosts drop the ball. To ensure you don't make the same mistake, leave every meeting with clear next steps.

I use a simple DOW framework:

- ***Due:*** What time and date is this due? (Don't use phrases such as 'ASAP'; be specific, especially when working across time-zones. Also, we all interpret ASAP quite differently.)
- ***Owner:*** Who owns the action?
- ***What:*** What exactly are they doing?

Book yourself out for 20 minutes after every meeting you host, so you have time to send out the summary and the actions.

Yes, this kind of admin after the meeting is boring work but when people know that your meetings always result in a clear follow-up, they trust the process. Plus, I find it easier to remember in the moment, rather than kicking the can a few days later, when it then really feels like a drag.

When you host meetings with a clear purpose, thoughtful casting, tight runtime, strong direction and clean follow-through, not only will you enjoy hosting more, but your meetings will also be more impactful.

Scene 17

Hosting a lunch and learn

A 'lunch and learn' is one of the lowest-risk, highest-return moves in this entire book. You pick a topic, you gather a small group and you create a conversation around it.

Before I started my consultancy, I was hosting scrappy little lunch and learns at work. These involved sitting around a table, or in front of a small group, and just sharing something I had recently figured out. Those sessions taught me how to facilitate a conversation, how to read a room and how to share what I knew using a variety of tools. They became the foundation for everything that followed.

Three things happen when you host a lunch and learn:

1. *You transfer knowledge:* You're sharing something genuinely useful with people who need it.
2. *You connect people:* A lunch and learn is often the only forum where people from different teams meet each other outside their team or project group. When you create that space, you become the connector. I always encourage people to bring a friend. Some of the best outcomes from a lunch and learn have nothing to do with the content and everything to do with the connections people make in the room.

3. *You practise in a low-stakes room:* You already know the topic, so you can focus on the hosting itself, such as how you start, how you read the room and how you bring people into the conversation.

Finding your topic

Often the best lunch and learns come from someone who is one or two steps ahead of everyone else. Here are three places to determine where you're a step or two ahead:

1. *Your Sent items:* Open your email and look at the questions you find yourself answering over and over. That repetition is a sign that this topic is in demand.
2. *Something you recently learned:* Maybe you've been experimenting with three AI tools that have helped you work faster? Maybe you've worked out a better approach to a process that was driving everyone mad? If you had to figure it out, others probably need to as well.
3. *Something you're curious about:* Pick whatever genuinely interests you right now, including a side-quest topic or something not directly related to your role. Some of the most popular lunch and learns I've seen have been side-quest topics — a finance person presenting on negotiation tactics, for example, or someone from IT walking through how they use AI to plan travel.

Your 50-minute structure

A typical lunch hour gives you about 50 minutes by the time people arrive and settle in. Here's my main rule for you when planning how to fill these 50 minutes: plan for only 15 to 20 minutes of actual content. The rest is conversation. I can't stress this enough. Packing 50 minutes of content into a 50-minute lunch and learn is a recipe for glazed eyes.

The following is a structure I use. (If you want more helpful workshop tips, read my first book, *The 2-Hour Workshop Blueprint: Design Fast. Deliver Strong. Without Stress.*)

Minutes 1 to 10: Set the scene

In the first ten minutes, welcome people, make them feel comfortable and find out why they are there.

If it's a small group, go around and ask, 'What are you curious about?' or 'Why did you come along today?' If it is a slightly larger group, get people to turn to the person next to them and share. If you're running this virtually, drop a prompt in the chat and give people a minute to respond.

Minutes 10 to 30: Share three key things

Rather than giving away 100 things, pick three things — for example, three lessons, three tools or three insights. Information overwhelm kills a lunch and learn faster than anything else.

You can deliver these three things in a variety of ways, such as through a story, through data or by sharing your screen and showing people how to do something. The key is to always connect each point back to why this is relevant for them and how it will improve their work or life.

For example, if I was doing a lunch and learn on my three favourite AI tools, I might pick one tool per point, show how I use it and then open the floor: 'Has anyone tried something similar? What is working for you?'

Minutes 30 to 45: Let people talk

Remember — people can search for content on their own. What they're really here for is how this is relevant to them in their business right now. They want your personal take, your specific experience within this company or industry, and to connect and talk to each other.

Provide two or three questions or prompts that they can discuss in pairs or trios, and then ask a spokesperson from each group to share back what resonated.

Minutes 45 to 50: Close with a question

Ask people to share what was most useful and what they would like to learn more about next time. Write those answers down. They give you the topic for your next session and insight into what this group needs.

If you can, grab a couple of quick testimonials from people who found the session useful. Even if they give you a sentence or two about what they took away, these comments help you promote your next sessions, and you can also store them as Work Receipts.

The title does 80 per cent of the work

Get the title for your lunch and learn right and people show up curious. Get it wrong and you're competing with their inbox.

I learnt this the hard way. Early in my career when I was marketing manager for a large training organisation, we renamed our 'Effective email management' course to 'Email hell to email heaven' and saw a surge in registrations.

Compare that with sessions I have run since:

- 'More than foot traffic: How to make your podiatry clinic famous.'

- '5 ways to ramp up the energy in your workshops (by being a bit lazy).'
- 'Why your employee engagement surveys are leading to divorce.'

Each of those titles does a few specific things. It creates a reaction. It speaks in the language the audience already uses. It has contrast or tension built into it. People read it and think, *I want to know the answer to that.*

If you can, include a number ('3 things', '5 ways') because it signals a structured, time-efficient session.

The content of your lunch and learn matters, obviously. But the title determines whether anyone is in the room to hear it.

Spread the word

What happens after your lunch and learn matters almost as much as the session itself. Here's how you can make the session even more powerful:

- *Capture the moment:* Take a group photo, a selfie or a quick behind-the-scenes shot of you running the lunch and learn. Share it online with a few key takeaways while the session is still fresh. This isn't Fight Club — don't not let the value stay trapped in the room.
- *Make it easy for the learning to travel:* A simple one-page cheat sheet sent to attendees afterwards can go a long way. Recap the main ideas, pull out a few practical actions and give people something they can forward to colleagues, or share links to resources mentioned. You can even include a line to encourage sharing, such as, 'If your team would benefit from a version of this, let me know'. People are far more likely to share something when the work has already been done for them.

- *Share the win internally:* Let your manager, your team and key stakeholders know what the session covered, what landed well and why it mattered. Too many people run a strong internal session and then act like it never happened. That is a missed opportunity. A lunch and learn is not just a learning moment. It is also proof that you're contributing, creating value and helping ideas move.

Capturing participant feedback while you're still in the room is also smart. When you ask people what they found most useful, pay attention to the exact words they use. Those phrases can become your workshop notes, future invitations, internal promotion or even the basis of coverage you later share more broadly.

You can also test demand before you leave. Ask a simple question like, 'Do you think this would be useful for other teams as well?' That one question can help you spot whether the session has legs beyond the original group.

Then do your own debrief. What worked? Where did the energy lift? What dragged? What questions came up that told you people wanted more? Every lunch and learn should make the next one better.

Work Fame in action

Steph Clarke

When Steph Clarke was 18 and only weeks into her audit career at EY (formerly Ernst & Young), she had an early glimpse of the work she really wanted to do. Sitting in a training session, she looked at the facilitator and thought, *I want to be the one up there.*

Rather than waiting for a formal opening in learning and development, she turned her current role into a rehearsal for the one she wanted. She saw an opportunity to help new graduates and interns joining the organisation, teaching them about the practicalities of a stocktake and some of the things she wished she'd known when she started—such as 'Wear flat shoes because you might be climbing ladders' and 'Yes, some of these stocktakes start at 7 am on New Year's Eve'.

For some sessions, she noticed content already existed in the business, so she'd take the slides and make them her own, always looking for ways to make dry material more fun.

Everything she taught came from being just far enough ahead to share what her time on the job had taught her—the kind of

(*continued*)

practical knowledge that someone newer would otherwise have to figure out alone. All of it sat outside her job description and built a track record in the career she wanted.

By the time formal opportunities in learning and development opened, Steph was first choice for the role. What started as volunteer lunch and learn sessions in a small Southampton office eventually led to her running workshops across 12 countries.

Enjoy hosting your session, and remember that all you need is something worth sharing and a room to share it in. Pick a topic you're interested in, find a room (even a virtual one), and invite a handful of people — that's all it takes to get started.

Scene 18

Making panels more powerful

While panels are usually something you attend, this scene is about becoming the person who runs them.

Think about what hosting a panel gives you in a single session: direct access to people who are usually impossible to reach, a seat on stage alongside the experts, and an audience that sees you as someone who belongs there.

One of my personal highlights was hosting a panel for Brisbane Roar FC, the football team I have supported for 20 years. Because I was the moderator, I was not just another fan in the stands. I was on stage being introduced alongside former Socceroos Matt McKay and Jade North, and former Matilda Elissia Carnavas.

Before the panel, I spent time going through their social media and recent posts, looking for stories they hadn't told a thousand times before. I even reached out to my friend Saji, who is even more football-obsessed than me, and asked him for question ideas.

Now picture yourself doing this in your industry — not as someone seeking advice from the people you admire, but as the person facilitating the conversation between them. How good would that be?! That's the moderator's seat, and it's available to you.

So, what separates a great moderator from someone who just happens to be holding the microphone? This scene is all about finding out.

Avoiding this hosting trap

We've all suffered through them — the sterile, predictable pattern where the moderator asks a generic question, panellist A gives a safe answer, panellist B nods and agrees, and panellist C essentially repeats what they both just said. The audience checks their phones. The energy flatlines.

Panels go flat when they turn into round-robin Q&A instead of a real conversation. Your job as host is to break that pattern. Mix up who responds to each question. Direct a specific question to one panellist. Leave someone out entirely when the question suits another voice better. Encourage the panellists to respond to each other, not just to you.

Quick tip: This type of conversation happens when you only have one microphone. Ideally, all panellists have a microphone but if you are limited, try to have at least two microphones (one for you and one for your panellists to share around). And remember — not every panellist needs to respond to every question.

The five Ps of panel hosting

To ensure your panel is memorable for the right reasons, I've developed a simple 5P framework.

Philosophy

Start with a theme that hints at a problem. Instead of 'Leadership excellence', for example, try 'The cost of playing it safe'. A sharper theme attracts a sharper audience — and sets the tone for a real conversation rather than a polished performance.

Your goal as moderator is to spark dialogue, not manage a sequence of individual answers. The worst panels are a string of 'I agree!' moments. The best ones have contrast, tension and the occasional moment where two panellists genuinely see things differently. If your philosophy is just 'get through the questions', you've already lost. Sometimes shaping the philosophy also means having a say on who the panellists are.

Preparation

Great moderators make it look effortless because they've done the serious work beforehand. Here's how you can do the same:

- *Skip the official bios:* Check recent interviews, social media posts and podcast appearances from the last six months. Look for patterns, contradictions and fresh angles. Has their perspective evolved? Do they hold unpopular opinions in their field? What are they wrestling with right now?
- *Craft introductions that land:* When I introduced Olympic legend Leisel Jones, I said, 'Between Leisel and I, we have won nine Olympic medals'. I then paused before adding, 'She won all nine'. It got a laugh (and was memorable).
- *Prepare twice as many questions as you think you will need:* Remember that your questions are conversation starters, not interview scripts. The best moderators know when to abandon their planned questions to follow where the discussion naturally wants to go.

Pre-briefing

You don't need an hour-long Zoom call with your panellist beforehand. A good email or quick two-minute video is enough.

Share some sample questions with a caveat: 'At times we may go off script, but these questions will help anchor the conversation'. Let them know you'll be encouraging them to banter with each other. And always ask if they have a project or something they would love you to mention in their intro.

Quick tip: For more on what to discuss with panellists beforehand, watch one of my panel pre-briefings at getworkfame.com/start.

Here's a briefing template you can also use.

> Hi *[panellist name],*
>
> I'm so excited to have you on the panel for *[event name]* on *[date].* My goal as your host is to make sure you look brilliant and that our audience walks away with insights they can't get anywhere else. The theme is *[x],* and I've listed some sample questions below as a primer.
>
> If you have an official bio or something you'd like me to share in your introduction, please send it through by *[date].*
>
> Here's a quick heads-up on how we'll host the conversation:
>
> - I won't be going down the line asking everyone the same question. I'll usually throw a question to one or two of you, and we'll take it from there.
> - If you've got a quick story, personal anecdote or experience, bring it into your response.
> - Feel free to jump in, build on each other's points, and have a bit of banter.
>
> Let me know if you have a specific project, book or 'win' you'd love for me to mention in your intro or during the wrap-up.
>
> Here are some sample questions; at times we may go off script, but these help to anchor in the conversation.

> *[Insert your questions here.]*
> Feel free to reach out if you have any questions.
> Thanks, see you then!

Performance

During the actual panel, you're juggling two roles: timekeeper and audience advocate.

Timekeeper

I use my Apple Watch set to buzz subtly on my wrist at the five-minute mark. You can't rely on glancing at your phone because it breaks your connection with the audience and signals to the panel that you might be tuning out of what they're saying. Alternatively, brief a colleague or friend in the audience to give you discrete hand signals at predetermined intervals.

It's also helpful to declare time boundaries up-front, using language like, 'We have exactly 30 minutes together. I'm committed to ending on time because I respect your schedules, and I'll make sure we cover the most important ground'.

You can use time boundaries as you close too, to signal last statements — for example, 'We're down to our final five minutes, so I'm going rapid-fire. One-sentence answers only …'

Audience advocate

You're the voice the audience doesn't have, so watch for energy signals such as the following:

- Heads nodding vigorously = lean into this topic.
- Glazed expressions = time to pivot immediately.
- Phone checking = inject energy or change direction.
- Forward leaning = they're hooked; dig deeper.

Also remember to trust your instincts. If you're feeling bored or confused, no doubt the audience is feeling that way too. You might need to move the conversation along using a segue — a smooth, uninterrupted transition from one topic or activity to another. In the following table, you'll find some example lines you can use to segue your panel conversation.

Using segues to keep a panel conversation on track

Intention	Example segue techniques
Go deeper	'I see a lot of nodding in the room, so I want to stay with this for a moment. Can you give us a specific example of what that looked like in practice?'
Translate or clarify	'Let me pause there. If you were explaining that to someone new to this topic, how would you say it?'
Change the angle	'I'm going to shift us slightly, because I want to bring this back to ... '
Pass between panellists	'I'm going to bring another voice in here. Priya, does that match what you've seen, or would you challenge it?'
Invite contrast	'Does anyone on the panel see this differently?'
Spotlight and extend	'I want to underline that phrase — "earning trust before you need it". Can you share more about what that means?'
Summarise and pivot	'So, what I'm hearing is: start smaller and build from there. Let's move from that idea into the question of what gets in the way.'

Quick tip: If a guest is rambling, just imagine that everyone in the audience wants you to steer the conversation back on track. Interrupt with a smile and say something like, 'Hey, can I just jump in on that? I'd love to get [*name's*] take on that specific point before we lose it ... '

Promotion

You've worked your way through your 4 Ps to organise your event, but make sure you don't forget one last P — promotion! Get the word out there for people who will be interested in attending, before, during and after the panel.

Before the panel

One easy way to promote the panel beforehand is a social media teaser, which you can post to LinkedIn or your internal work channels. Try something like the following:

> What happens when you put *[panellist 1]*, *[panellist 2]*, and *[panellist 3]* in a room to talk about *[theme]*?
>
> I've been obsessed with the idea of *[specific topic]* lately. So, I decided to stop wondering and start asking.
>
> On *[date]*, I'm hosting a special panel at *[event name]* to dive deep into:
>
> - *[Insight 1; for example, 'Why traditional strategy is dead']*
> - *[Insight 2; for example, 'The secret to making faster decisions']*
>
> I'll be joined by *[tag panellist 1]*, *[tag panellist 2]*, and *[tag panellist 3]*.
>
> Want to join us? Grab your spot here: *[link]*

During the panel

Capture everything. Obviously, this is hard to do when you're on stage, but I highly recommend asking a friend or colleague to snap photos and videos during the panel. Also, don't forget the behind-the-scenes content. Try capturing the green room chat, the sound check and the moment when your panellists meet each other for the first time — sometimes this is more fun to capture than the actual conversation.

After the panel

Your panel content can fuel weeks of social media posts and professional conversations. You can create quote graphics featuring the best insights from the session, for example, and tag your panellists — they'll likely share them, extending your reach to their networks. Or you can write a reflection post about what surprised you most from the conversation.

Also make sure you send a personalised thankyou message to each panellist within 24 hours. Include a photo from the event and mention a specific moment that stood out. Keep your message short and genuine.

Hosting a panel is one of the fastest ways to prove you belong in the room with the best in your industry. The audience sees you as a peer of the panellists, and that perception stays with them long after the event ends.

Scene 19

The conference strategy

Conferences, industry events and company offsites are some of the best chances you'll get all year to meet new people. I love going to them but also recognise that sometimes the opportunities they offer are easy to squander. You show up, sit through sessions, add a few people on LinkedIn, have some fun chats at networking drinks and then head home. A few weeks later, you might not remember a single name.

This scene is about doing conferences and events differently.

In two days, you can make more meaningful connections than you might in two months at your desk. You get a window into what's really happening in your industry — what others are working on, what concerns them and what excites them — and that outside view is genuinely valuable to bring back to your team. It sharpens your thinking, gives you new ideas and gives you something worth talking about.

The people who get the most out of conferences don't leave it to chance. They show up with a strategy. So, let's figure out a new strategy to make the best out of the time you've committed.

Working out where to invest your time

Your time is limited, and you can't attend every conference and industry event on offer. You first need to decide what return you're after and whether you should attend at all.

What's the ROI?

Before committing funding and time away from work for you to attend any event, conference or training program, someone always asks, 'What's the return on investment (ROI)?' It is a totally fair question. I ask myself the same thing.

Sure, you can review the event outcomes and say, 'As a result of attending this, I am going to increase my income tenfold', or 'I will learn how to use AI to reduce my working hours to two hours a day and retire next month'.

But those promises are not real, because the return you get from any event is up to you. It depends on what you do, who you meet and what you take away from the experience.

Two people can attend the exact same conference and get very different returns from it. One might leave with a handful of new LinkedIn connections and some great travel footage for Instagram Stories. The other leaves with a powerful new relationship, a fresh idea they've already started acting on and a reputation that's a little more lit up than when they arrived.

Once you've decided an event is worth attending, don't outsource your ROI to the organisers. That part is on you.

Should you attend?

Not every conference is worth your time or money. Before you commit, do a quick sense-check: is this where your industry actually gathers? Who is running the event and can you genuinely learn from the speakers? Is the audience one you want to be part of? If the answer to those questions is yes, go. If you're only going because it's on the calendar or someone else suggested it, think again.

One way to figure this out is to ask someone you trust. This is a great question to use when you're reaching out to people you admire or connecting with your friendtors: 'I want to get better at *[topic]*. Which conferences do you recommend I attend?'

If you don't have someone to ask, do your own homework. Check the event's Instagram or LinkedIn page. Jump on the website. Look at the photos and videos from previous years. What is the vibe?

Also check out the seating plan. If everyone is sitting in a grand hall facing the front all day, with no breakouts, no social networking time built into the program and no opportunities to speak to others, consider whether you would prefer to watch a video or the YouTube channel of their key speakers.

Finally, think about whether the content matches where you're headed. Once you have done that due diligence and decided it is worth going, then the strategy outlined in the remainder of this scene kicks in.

Before the event

Here are some tips for getting the most out of the event before you even get there:

- *Research the lineup:* Check the speaker list and, if available, the attendee list. Identify three to five people you want to meet — these might come straight from your Quest list (refer to scene 11).
- *Reach out beforehand:* Send a short message to the three to five people you've identified. Say something like, 'I'll be at *[event]* and would love to say hello. I've been following

your work on *[topic]* and would value a quick conversation if you have a few minutes between sessions'. The same principles from 'How to reach out (the right way)' (scene 13) apply here: specificity, a personal hook and a contained ask. A connection request that mentions you're attending the same event puts you on someone's radar before you arrive.

- *Organise your own side quest:* Consider hosting a dinner, coffee or walk outside the official program. You could also arrange a small gathering for contacts in that city who aren't attending the event.
- *Decide your output before you go:* Block some time in after the event to follow through on any learnings or insights. Committing to it before you arrive means you're already planning to act on what you learn.

During the event

Here's how to boost your ROI during the event:

- *Adopt host energy:* Even as an attendee, you can introduce people to each other, ask the first question after a talk and be the person who turns a group of strangers into a group of colleagues.
- *Ask the question:* After a session, put your hand up where appropriate. Alternatively, take the opportunity to catch up with the speaker after the session, and share what resonated with you the most (speakers *love* hearing this!).
- *Don't eat alone:* Lunch, coffee breaks and the walk between sessions are where the real conversations happen. Sit with people you don't know. Introduce yourself. Ask what brought them to the event and what they're excited to work on next.

- *Volunteer:* Offer to introduce a speaker, host a table discussion or summarise key takeaways for the group. Really listen to the questions other people are asking. Pay attention to how they describe their challenges and opportunities. This provides you with good intelligence on what is going on in your industry.

After the event

Lock in your learnings with the following:

- *Follow up within 48 hours:* Send a personal message to everyone you had a good conversation with. Skip the generic 'Great to meet you'. Instead, say something specific, like, 'I have been thinking about your point on *[topic]*. Here is a resource that connects to it'. Or: 'I really valued our conversation about *[topic]*. Would love to keep talking. Are you open to a 15-minute call next week?'
- *Stay a little bit longer (if work allows):* If you're travelling, even taking one extra day helps you process what you learned and plan your next steps before going back to your usual routine. If the event is local, try to block off some time in your calendar the day after for the same reason.
- *Share the love:* Talk about what you learned with someone who was not at the event. Explaining it to a coworker or friend helps you figure out your main takeaways. You can do this in person or by writing a post or presenting a summary of the conference key learnings to your team or company.
- *Update your connection map:* Add new names to your Best, Test and Quest lists while they're fresh.

Bonus: Attending networking events

While we're here talking about conferences, we might as well dovetail into chatting about the usual day-to-day networking events in your town, hosted by an industry or association.

When you hear the words 'networking event', what comes to mind? Is it small talk, forced smiles and the urge to check your phone every five minutes? It doesn't have to be this way. Networking events are a great way to meet new people. Here are some tips to help you get the most out of them.

Firstly, should you go?

If you're new to a job, just starting out, or in a new city or industry, try to attend as many events as possible. This helps you get a sense of what these events are like, who goes and what the vibe is. You won't know until you try, and you never know who you'll meet. As you gain experience, you'll get better at knowing which events are worth your time. The more you attend, the easier it becomes to trust your instincts.

A question I like to ask myself when I look at an event before RSVPing is this: 'If it were raining and the event was tonight, would I still want to go?' And once you have said you'll go, do your absolute best to show up — not showing up after RSVPing sends the wrong message.

Networking the right way

Have you clicked 'Attend'? Great! Go in with the mindset of making one other person feel comfortable. I always feel relieved when someone comes over and says hello first — so be that person for others. Walk up to someone and start with a question. You're not the only one there on your own.

Remember — a successful networking event isn't about collecting as many LinkedIn connections as possible and leaving exhausted. One or two real conversations is enough. Choose quality over quantity, every time.

Here are a few practical tactics that help:

- *Stand near the food or drinks:* It makes starting conversations easier and gives you something to do with your hands.
- *Put your phone away:* Looking down makes you less approachable and gives you an easy out, which defeats the purpose of being there.
- *Act like a mini host:* Say hello, introduce people to each other or help someone who looks like they're standing alone feel more at ease. If you see someone on their own, go over and just say, 'Hi! It's my first time here, what about you?' or 'What brought you tonight?'
- *If a conversation runs its course, it's fine to move on:* Say something like, 'It was great chatting — I'm going to say hello to a few others, but let's connect'. People understand. It's a networking event.
- *Make connecting in the moment easy:* You don't need a business card, but having your LinkedIn app on your phone means you can quickly find someone and connect with them in the moment. When you do that, bonus points if you can write a quick, 'Hi, great to meet you at *[event name]*!' message — because a few months later, you might forget how you met this person, and having that original message is a great prompt.

Go one level deeper: Volunteering or joining the committee

Attending a conference puts you in the room. Helping to organise one puts you at the centre of it.

Most industry conferences, professional associations and membership bodies run on the back of volunteer committees, and they are almost always looking for people to contribute. Committees, advisory boards, awards panels and working groups all need members who are engaged, reliable and invested in the industry.

The access this creates is different from anything you get as an attendee. You're working alongside the organisers, the speakers and the decision-makers before the event even begins. You have a legitimate reason to reach out to people, a visible role in shaping the agenda and a front-row seat to the conversations your industry is having.

If you want to go further, look at the professional associations relevant to your field and check whether they have committees or volunteer programs. If nothing is listed publicly, reach out and ask. Committee members are genuinely grateful when someone puts their hand up to get involved.

Conferences and networking events are only as useful as what you do with them. Have a plan before you go, show up with intention and follow through afterwards.

Spotlight check: Conversations

Congrats on making it to this point! Let's pause here before moving on.

The Conversations spotlight has been about the people around you—the ones who know you, remember you, mention your name, make introductions and think of you at the right moment. Your work doesn't travel on its own. It gets carried through conversations, built on trust, and shaped by dozens of small interactions that didn't feel significant at the time.

Those conversations are happening; the question is whether you're in them.

Rate this spotlight

On a scale of 1 to 10, how bright is your Conversations spotlight right now? Rate yourself based on the following:

- *1:* I mostly keep my head down, talk to the same people and hope the right opportunities somehow find me.
- *10:* I'm building strong relationships, staying in people's worlds and my name is moving through rooms I'm not in.

Write your number down. What would it look like if you were one to two points higher? What would you do differently?

Three questions to reflect on

Sit with the following questions to reflect on how to increase your Conversations spotlight:

1. *Who is likely to mention your name when you're not in the room?* What would they say and is that what you want them to say?
2. *Which relationship have you let drift?* Who did you mean to stay in touch with but haven't?
3. *Where are you still letting hierarchy live rent-free in your head?* Who have you decided is too senior, too important or too far away to reach out to—and is that actually true?

Spotlight three

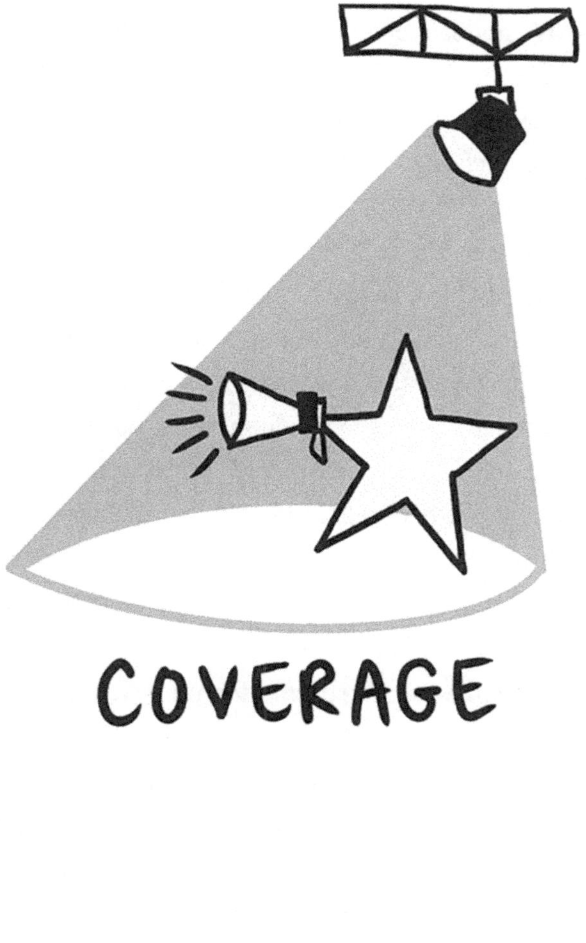

Welcome to your third and final Work Fame spotlight. Coverage is about sharing your ideas widely, so you become known in your industry and beyond. It allows your ideas and expertise to reach people you haven't met yet.

Until you start sharing your ideas broadly, your professional reputation is limited. It only extends to those who have met you, worked with you or heard about you from others.

A single post, podcast episode or even comment on someone else's article can reach people you've never met, in places you've never been, inside organisations you've never heard of. I've connected with people across the globe because they heard my podcast or found something I posted. Those opportunities never would have happened through meetings and coffees alone.

Now, you might think that having a huge network on LinkedIn is the golden ticket to getting noticed. Yes, a strong network (quantity) is fantastic but quality is also important. Recent research from Joanna Davis and colleagues dove deep into how people use LinkedIn and discovered that it wasn't the sheer number of connections someone had that led to career boosts. What truly made a difference was how frequently someone used the platform — that is, how often they actively engaged, shared their insights, posted articles and celebrated their achievements.[16]

Further data from LinkedIn reveals a startling 'content deficit' that works in your favour. While the platform's reach is immense, with 9 billion impressions generated every week, the actual number of people creating that content is remarkably small — estimated at just 1 per cent of the monthly active user base.[17] This means that by simply showing up and sharing your ideas, you're immediately entering the top 1 per cent of the most visible professionals on the planet.

Posting your coverage creates an online legacy of your thinking, separate from your employer. When people search for you, they'll find evidence that you're thoughtful, proactive and invested in your industry.

Scene 20

The thought breeder mindset

'But Leanne! I'm not a thought leader.' Good. Neither am I — and you don't need to be.

For me, being a 'thought leader' implies having a fully formed, defensible, original point of view on a topic, ideally supported by data, wrapped in a framework, and delivered with the confidence of someone who has been thinking about it longer and harder than everyone else in the world. That's a *lot* of pressure for someone who just noticed something interesting at work and wants to share it, hoping it might help others.

So, I decided to lower the pressure. Instead of calling myself a thought leader, I became a 'thought breeder'. A thought breeder notices things, captures ideas and shares them before they go cold. They post half-formed observations, real stories and practical insights that could help others — basically, they put ideas into the world and see what grows.

Here's how I see the two modes operate:

- *The thought leader:* In this mode, you're thinking deeply, noting ideas and frequently publishing your own concepts. Some prominent experts operate here; they observe their environment but deliberately tune out the noise of others to focus entirely on pushing out their own content. Sometimes, you have to enter this mode, shutting off external inputs to create the space needed to connect different pieces of information and make sense of what is going on.

- *The thought breeder:* Here you do not just consume ideas; you also convert them. You read widely and listen closely, spot patterns and connect dots. Then, you put those connections into the world. You share, publish, test and refine your ideas through feedback.

The following table provides a summary of how a thought breeder operates differently from a traditional thought leader.

The difference between being a thought leader and a thought breeder

Thought leader	Thought breeder
Shares polished ideas	Generates ideas in public
Publishes when certain	Thinks out loud
Operates with authority	Operates with curiosity
Delivers finished frameworks	Experiments with half-formed thoughts
Teaches from hindsight	Learns in real time
Builds status through answers	Builds interest through questions
Waits until the thinking is 'ready'	Captures and shares while the thinking is alive

When I reframed myself as a thought breeder, everything got easier. I started sharing what I was noticing, testing and learning. Some of those ideas turned into keynotes and some became frameworks.

I started my podcast, *First Time Facilitator*, because I was leading workshops and had no idea what I was doing. I couldn't find any useful podcasts on facilitation, so I made the show I wished existed. That's the thought breeder mindset. You notice a gap, a question or something useful, and instead of waiting for someone more qualified to say it, you go first.

Quick tip: If you're thinking about something, someone else probably is too. Even an audience of one is enough to begin. Start now and let your ideas find the people who need them.

Separate yourself from your idea

There's you, and there's your idea. They're separate.

You're a person with interests, quirks, opinions, stories, skills, contradictions and probably a few mildly unhinged obsessions.

An idea is just one thing that you present. People can disagree with it, ignore it, challenge it, love it or scroll past it, but their reaction to the idea is about the idea, and it's separate from your value as a person.

Tying your self-worth to how many 'likes' your post gets is dangerous. When you separate yourself from your ideas, everything changes. You can put an idea into the world, see what happens and move on.

While your likes and views are not your worth, they can teach you what resonates with your readers. Every post gives you data about what sparks conversation. You cannot get that intelligence without sharing your work. Treat the metrics as feedback, not a verdict.

In the following sections, I run through some more objections I hear to sharing your thoughts more widely — and how I counter them.

'What if my boss, or Bob from accounting sees it?'

That great! Being seen is all part of the fame experience. Most of the time, people are supportive or inspired, or they simply move on with their day. The more you post, the easier it gets. Eventually, you realise sharing your ideas online is not nearly as scary, or as significant, as it feels in your head.

You will quickly find that people don't care as much as you think they do. When I am on LinkedIn, the amount of scrolling I do makes it hard to capture my attention. Psychologists call this the spotlight effect: we overestimate how much people notice and judge our posts, when they are really focused on their own lives and feeds.

Of course, stay clear of anything that would embarrass your employer, could be defamatory or could reflect poorly on you — for example, politically charged messages. But keep in mind that the real challenge is getting people to care enough to stop scrolling. That's where you can use the pattern interrupt strategies you learnt in back in scene 7 (in the Contribution spotlight).

'I have nothing to say/everything has already been said'

When you say, 'I have nothing to say', what you really mean is you don't yet trust that what you have to say is valuable. That's normal, but rarely true. You're underestimating your real-life experience. Someone a few steps behind you, beside you or even ahead of you in a different context can benefit from your perspective.

If you've solved a problem, spotted a pattern, tried a new tool, changed your mind, asked a good question or noticed a common tension, you have something worth sharing.

Also, it is true that very little is completely original. But it hasn't been said by you, through your lens, with your stories, for this audience, at this time. Your perspective is the value.

'Posting is cringe'

Sure, humble bragging disguised as reflection is definitely cringe. But sharing a genuine perspective on something you care about, in your real voice, with a specific example? Writing about your favourite tech tool that saves you a tonne of work? That's helpful!

'My work is confidential'

Think about what questions you're getting every day in your job. What are the problems that keep coming up? Those are the things people want to know about. You're not posting about the restructure, the acquisition or the internal strategy document. You're posting about the craft of your work and how you approach problems. (For more in this area, see scene 27.)

More than just posts

I want to emphasise one more thing before we dive into the rest of this spotlight. Coverage includes LinkedIn posts, yes. But it also includes articles, podcast episodes, speaking at events, contributing to industry publications and sharing your perspective in any public forum.

For now, believe this: your ideas deserve to be heard, and the rest of this part will show you exactly how to make that happen.

Scene 21

The Coverage Gym

If the idea of 'putting yourself out there' makes you want to suddenly remember you have laundry to fold, let's lower the pressure.

The Coverage Gym is here to help you build your sharing muscle before you go big. You can start small, build confidence and get more comfortable sharing your thoughts online.

In this scene, we start with two things:

1. making sure your profile is working for you
2. choosing a level of engagement that feels manageable, so you can build confidence before you build reach.

Checking your profile

Start with the basics and check what you've included in your LinkedIn profile. If needed, return to your work receipts folders from scene 8 (in the Contribution spotlight) and borrow from the language and feedback you've collected.

Next, complete an eight-minute profile audit. Open your profile and pretend you're seeing it for the first time. Ask yourself:

- 'Do I have a clear, recent photo?'
- 'Does my headline say more than my job title?'
- 'Does my experience section focus on results rather than just tasks?'

- 'Have I featured anything that shows my thinking or work achievements?'
- 'Does my activity show signs of life?'
- 'Can people easily work out what I am known for?'
- 'Do I sound like an actual human?'
- 'Have I shown the work I want to be known for?'

If you need to update your LinkedIn tagline, here are three formats you can follow:

1. *What you do + who it helps:* I help *[who]* do *[what]*. Examples of this format include:
   - 'I help leaders communicate clearly when the stakes are high.'
   - 'I help teams create better meetings, workshops, and events.'
2. *Role + area of expertise: [Role] | [specialty], [topic you care about]*. For example:
   - 'HR leader | Culture, capability and future of work.'
   - 'Project manager | Stakeholder engagement, delivery and influence.'
3. *Role + value created: [Role]* helping *[group]* achieve *[result]*. For example:
   - 'Finance leader helping teams make better commercial decisions.'
   - 'Operations manager helping frontline teams work smarter and safer.'

Three levels of social media engagement

I came up with the Coverage Gym framework because diving headfirst into posting can feel like walking into a gym for the first time and trying to lift the heaviest barbell you see. It's always smarter to warm up instead. Start easy and then level up as you get stronger.

React (light weights)

This is the warm-up. Like, celebrate or react to other people's posts. It takes about two seconds and does a few things at once:

- *It keeps you on other people's radar:* Your face and name appear in their notifications. This is a simple way to stay on people's minds, which links back to what we covered in the Conversations spotlight. It is an easy, low-pressure way to keep in touch without having to send a message each time.
- *It trains you to notice what draws you in:* Pay attention to what makes you hit that button. The posts that spark a reaction give you clues about what you care about. When something creates a genuine reaction, screenshot it or save it, and then click the notification bell on that person's profile so you see their future posts. These can give you fuel for later comments and later posts. See what types of posts you like and resonate with, and use that as inspiration for your own coverage down the track.
- *It can open doors you did not expect:* Even if you simply react, people might see who you are and reach out to you. It works the other way, too. You might see someone's post on LinkedIn and, instead of reacting publicly, decide to send them a direct message about it. Try something like, 'I just saw your post about *x*, and it really resonated'. That is a private, personal way of starting a conversation, and it often lands even more meaningfully than a public comment because the person knows you took the extra step to reach out one on one.

Jump in as an observer and get a feel for the landscape. After a couple of weeks of light reps, commenting will feel far less intimidating.

Comment (medium weights)

Commenting is where you start adding your thoughts to someone else's conversation, and it has two levels:

- *Simple and generous commenting:* This involves giving kudos and acknowledgement. 'Great job on this.' 'This is really exciting, congratulations.' 'Sharp take, especially the point about ...' This kind of commenting is an easy way to ease in, and it still counts because your name and your face are showing up in a professional context.
- *Adding your own perspective to the conversation:* This type of commenting is more like improv — you want to add to what is already there, not just applaud it. For example:
  - 'Here is what we saw on our side ...'
  - 'Here is what I think about that ...'
  - 'I read something recently that connects to this ...'

What makes a comment memorable is specificity — for example, a practical example from your own experience or a concrete detail that shows you're not just agreeing in the abstract. 'We had the same challenge and here is what we did' is worth ten 'Great post!' reactions.

You can grow your LinkedIn following significantly just by being thoughtful in your commenting. LinkedIn promotes good comments, and they get a lot of eyeballs. Other people see your comments, see how thoughtful they are and might connect with you because of them.

Quick tip: If you see something that made you want to comment, save it as well. Copy your comments into your Notes app. Your comments often become the seeds of your own posts. You might look back at a comment you wrote three weeks ago and think, *That is actually a full post waiting to happen.*

Post (heavy weight)

Sharing your own original thinking is the big lift. Your post might be a story from your week, a lesson you learned, a question you're wrestling with or a perspective on something happening in your industry.

I cover exactly how to do this in the scenes that follow, including finding your voice and inspiration, writing a hook that earns the click and building a rhythm that doesn't take over your life.

Shifting from commenting to posting often happens naturally. You will be writing a comment and realise you have more to say than fits in a reply. You might want to go into more detail, add more examples, bring in more of your perspective and perhaps add a story to it. That's a great moment to turn your comment into a post.

Every rep counts

You don't need to go heavy during every session at the Coverage Gym. Some weeks, you'll feel inspired to post your idea; other weeks, you'll stick to a few comments and some reactions. The point is to keep showing up.

And on the days where posting feels like too much, you can always drop back to the lighter weights, as with any good workout — mix it up!

Scene 22

Establishing your voice

My friend Andrew Hollo writes an excellent newsletter. Every week, I read it and feel a little jealous. He pulls in history, studies and sharp references that somehow make you feel smarter by the end of the piece. Part of me would love to write like that. Then I remember, *Leanne, you're not Andrew.*

So instead of trying to sound like him, I lean into what sounds like me — everyday moments, stories from work and things I think about while out running. That's where my voice lives.

Your voice lives in the equivalent place for you.

'But I am not that unique!'

If you can't hear your own voice clearly, it's likely because you're too close to it. You don't notice the phrases you repeat, the references you always reach for or the way you naturally tell a story. To you, it all feels normal. To everyone else, it stands out. You just need to understand what makes it unique.

Your 'voice' encompasses the words and phrases you use to communicate in everyday life. The problem is that we tend to disconnect from our own voice when we go online. We try to change how we write things to make our message sound more impressive or more professional. What that does is flatten everything, though. People connect with people, and a lot of the content that cuts through on LinkedIn feels like it was written by a human.

It's hard to escape the 'write professionally' trap. I think it took me about 12 months to start writing in a way that reflects who I am. In this scene, I share how I got there, so hopefully it won't take you as long.

Quick tip: Bring that 'thought breeder' mindset from scene 20 into your voice as well.

Why voice matters

A lot of what feels cringeworthy on LinkedIn is not the act of posting; it's that people sound beige and vanilla because they have corporatised their own personalities out of their writing. When others read your writing and it sounds like something you would say in real life, your post feels more relatable.

Here are two quick exercises that will help you uncover your voice.

Your voice audit (10 minutes)

This exercise turns you into a detective of your own communication style. Grab a pen, open your phone and work through these five steps:

1. *Check your sent messages:* Open your texts or WhatsApp and scroll through recent conversations with friends, family and close colleagues. Notice your repeated greetings, sign-offs, reactions and favourite expressions. How do you say yes when you're excited? How do you respond to good news? How do

you end a conversation? Everyone has words and phrases they use without thinking about it. Some of mine include: '11/10', 'Amaze', 'High five'. What are yours?

2. *Look at your recently used emojis:* That row of recently used is a personality snapshot. Mine tells you plenty: dog, fire, palm tree, blue heart. Write down your top three.
3. *Uncover your reactions:* Think about the last time someone told you something brilliant. What came out of your mouth? Maybe it was 'Get out of here!' 'That is unreal' or 'Tell me everything'.
4. *Think about your references:* When you explain something casually, where does your brain go for examples? Sport? Films? Travel? Music? Food? These go-to references are part of your voice.
5. *Find your rants:* What topics get you fired up? What could you talk about for ten minutes with no preparation? Lazy communication? Terrible design? Your frustrations often reveal your strongest voice.

The documentary of you (10 minutes)

Imagine a camera crew has been following you around for the past month. They have filmed everything: your work life and your weekends. Now they are editing it all into a short documentary about you.

On a fresh page, write down what makes the final cut.

- *The work scenes:* What moments would they keep cutting back to? Perhaps sketching ideas on napkins during meetings? Making people laugh in the middle of a tense conversation? Teaching yourself how to code? Write those scenes down.

- *The after-hours scenes:* What would they film outside of work? For me, it's completing a Peloton workout, re-watching Tom Cruise movies for the hundredth time and sending a voice note from the dog park. What are your interests and passions?

This material helps to personalise your posts.

Using your voice

Once you've completed the voice audit and the documentary exercise, your next focus is bringing this into your coverage.

Start with your favourite phrases from the voice audit. These are your go-to ways of responding in comments or reactions. Instead of writing 'This is fantastic', for example, or 'I'm so proud of you' (generic lines that could come from anyone), reply how you would in real life. For example, I'll write 'I 11/10 love this new tech tool'. It's just the way I talk.

Next, look at your favourite emojis. I use the palm tree emoji a lot because I love tropical weather. I sign off my Work Fame newsletter by putting a palm tree at the end of my signature. It's a small detail but completely me.

With the documentary exercise, look for ways to weave those scenes into your posts. I regularly drop Tom Cruise into my coverage because I genuinely admire his commitment to his craft — so when I'm making a point about going all in, he's the reference that pops up. I also talk about my Peloton rides, my sausage dog and rooftop bars. These details make my coverage mine. People get to know you as a person, and that's what makes your posts real and relatable.

Work Fame in action

Fathia Tayib

Fathia Tayib is a public policy professional specialising in privacy and responsible AI. She is also a powerful example of what happens when you stop trying to sound like everyone else and start sharing your unique perspective.

For a long time, Fathia was a silent lurker on LinkedIn. She posted maybe two or three times a year, and only the standard, template-driven corporate update: 'I've started a new job' or 'I've completed a course'. It was short, a bit boring and, most importantly, it didn't sound like her. In real life, her brain moves fast and she speaks with passion. Online, she had flattened all of that out.

But while she wasn't posting much, she was connecting. She intentionally sought out people who shared her interests, in Australia and globally. She connected with angel investors, space exploration enthusiasts, and women of colour leading the privacy and responsible AI space in the United States. Seeing how these women wrote and the impact they had inspired her. She realised

(*continued*)

she didn't just want to consume their ideas; she wanted to bring those conversations to Australia.

So, she started writing. She started sharing her ideas on LinkedIn before creating a Substack to explore privacy and AI ethics through the lens of her lived experience. She stopped using the corporate templates and started leaning into what made her different.

When people tell Fathia they aren't unique enough to have a voice, she gives them this advice: draw a Venn diagram. In one circle, put your professional expertise. In the second, your lived experience. In the third, your interests and passions. The place where all three overlap? That's your voice.

For Fathia, that overlap meant writing about the privacy implications of AI tools designed to help with executive dysfunction—combining her expertise in privacy, her lived experience as a neurodivergent person and her passion for responsible tech. This was content only she could write.

The opportunities that followed from sharing her ideas publicly were significant. She was approached to judge the Women in AI Asia–Pacific Awards, twice. She was invited to attend closed-door seminars and conferences she would never have accessed otherwise. She received speaking opportunities, advisory board invitations and recruiter outreach, all through her LinkedIn and Substack presence.

She became the first Australian to participate in the Google Responsible Innovation Fellowship, a connection made through LinkedIn's algorithm. And her writing became evidence in job and board interviews—proof of a long-term, genuine commitment to her field, not just a line on a CV.

As Fathia says, 'If you are human, you are unique. Put your ideas out there. Don't let your fears and doubts stop you'.

How to write like you

Here is the process I use to write in my voice:

1. *Get the idea out:* Go for a walk or just open your voice notes and talk through what is on your mind. Give yourself a question to answer and just talk. You can create a transcript of that and then shape it up from there. This captures your authentic voice — the actual lines you would say — before your brain has a chance to corporatise them.
2. *Add your personal flair:* Once your idea is on the page, the uplevel is about 20 per cent effort: zhuzhing it with a personal reference, an emoji of yours, an example from your documentary scenes or a phrase from your voice audit. You're personalising the post so it could only have come from you.
3. *Read it out loud before you post:* This is the simplest quality check there is. If you wouldn't say the words to a friend over coffee, adjust them until you would. If it sounds like a press release or a corporate update, rewrite it until it sounds like you talking. Honestly, read it out loud. I don't have too many 'rules' but that is one of them, especially as you're getting started.

Once you know your phrases, use them in your online writing. Please stop editing them out in the name of 'professionalism'.

Scene 23

What Work Famous people reveal online

If you work inside a large organisation, you might assume this spotlight is not for you. Maybe you think posting on LinkedIn is for consultants, coaches and people who need to promote their business. If you're in the corporate world, the thought of posting on LinkedIn may even give you the 'ick'.

But for Liz Heathwood, this view creates a missed opportunity. Liz is a senior HR leader who has built a strong reputation while working inside large organisations. She spotted something many corporate professionals avoid: your brand on the outside of your organisation matters as much as it does on the inside. Improving your Coverage spotlight may feel uncomfortable at first, but it's a muscle that can be built.

As Liz shared with me, 'I like being seen as good at what I do, and that I bring not only an internal perspective but also an external perspective to the work. If you want to be thinking about what's ahead, looking around the corner, you can't just live in your bubble. This is what will set you apart from others'.

In part through sharing her thinking publicly on platforms such as LinkedIn, Liz was invited to join the industry advisory board for the University of Queensland's human resources program, she has appeared on podcasts, and she has been a guest speaker at conferences and internal organisation events. For someone who did not start out in HR, these are proud moments for Liz, reflecting the reputation she had built beyond her job title.

Liz believes that a huge opportunity exists to learn from others inside organisations. 'Many of us are experiencing the same things, but we don't talk about it. I understand the fear of feeling like you are talking out of school. But you can share in a way that is still respectful and positive while maintaining confidentiality.'

Your perspective from the inside is more valuable than you think. It provides an opportunity for you to stand out and be seen as an expert at what you do. For Liz it's not about the 'likes'; the benefits come when people in her network reach out behind the scenes and say how much they appreciate what she talks about.

Before I show you what this can look like, remember the thought breeder mindset from scene 20. You are not stepping onto a stage to deliver a perfect monologue. You are opening a conversation.

You can do that in three simple ways: curate, create and chronicle.

Curate

When you curate, you act as a filter. You share someone else's idea and add your perspective to it. This is the lowest-effort, lowest-risk form of coverage, and a brilliant place to start because you're not starting from scratch. You're reacting to something that already exists and showing people how you think.

Liz told me colleagues in her organisation often come to her and ask, 'We've got something happening on *x*. Who should we talk to?'

Over time, she has built a mental Rolodex from the people she follows, the podcasts she listens to and the ideas she keeps tabs on.

One time, her team were talking about the need for a facilitator in Reykjavík (the capital of Iceland), and Liz said, 'Actually, I know someone in Reykjavík'. Her leader's reply: 'Of course you do!'

Here are some tips to get you started with curating content:

- Share something from your industry or the latest relevant research, and then break this down into practical steps for how you would apply it in an organisation. This shows that you can take abstract thinking and make it practical and demonstrates subject matter expertise.
- Share a podcast, article or talk and explain the one idea that stayed with you, and how you have been thinking about it or applying it to the work that you do.
- Tag the creator/thought leader and say why their work matters.
- Share the top five books that have changed your career (and tag the authors!).
- Spotlight a colleague's thinking or contribution, and comment on why it's important.
- Share a quote and add, 'Here's what this made me think about in my own work'.

Create

When you create, you put your own thinking into the world. This is where you stop simply passing on ideas and start shaping them.

Some starting points for you to consider:

- *How your thinking has changed over time:* For example, 'I used to think *x*; now I think *y*'. This works because it shows your thinking moving. People trust people who are willing to admit they have changed their mind.

- *Something you have explained a few times this month:* This shows interest exists in the question, and maybe other people would like to hear your response too.
- *A question someone asked you that made you stop and think:* Share the question and your answer.
- *A trend in your industry that is overhyped or underestimated:* Say what you think and where you believe attention should go instead.
- *A lesson from your own career:* For example, 'Ten years ago I was doing *x*. Here's what I understand now that I did not understand then'.

Chronicle

When you chronicle, you're letting people into your working life as it happens. This is the easiest type of content because you're just documenting what you're already doing. For example, when I would visit different offices in my organisation around the world, I'd take selfies with colleagues and post them on social media, sharing what I learnt during the trip.

Liz does this well. 'I've led projects that have been really challenging', she told me, 'and I share what made them difficult, along with lessons learned along the way and tips on how to make them better'.

When you chronicle your working life, you might share:

- a behind-the-scenes look at how you approached a tricky problem
- an overview of something you're building, testing or improving
- a challenge you're working through
- an event, workshop or meeting that sparked a useful insight
- a lesson learned halfway through a piece of work, not just at the polished end.

Make the first line earn the click

You could have the most useful, interesting, original post in the world, but it doesn't matter if nobody reads past the first line.

According to UC Irvine professor Gloria Mark, whose research has tracked screen behaviour and attention spans over two decades, we spend an average of just 47 seconds on any screen before our attention shifts.[18] On a fast-moving feed such as LinkedIn, that window is even shorter. People see the first two lines of your post before they must hit the 'see more' button. This means those two lines need to do one job: make the reader curious enough to keep going.

In what behavioural economist George Loewenstein calls 'information gap theory', this curiosity arises the moment people sense a gap between what they know and what they want to know.[19] A great opening line doesn't give people information; it also reveals a gap. Once that gap is opened, an almost irresistible drive emerges to close it.

Here are some examples of opening lines that encourage readers to click 'see more' and read the rest of your post:

- 'I have been in my role for six years and I only just figured out ... '
- 'I'm 42. The single best financial move I made happened at 28, and it had nothing to do with ... '
- 'Everyone in my industry talks about *[common thing]*. Almost nobody talks about *[uncommon thing]*.'
- 'I have had 32 one-on-one meetings this quarter. Here is the one question I ask in every single one.'
- 'Last Tuesday at 3 pm I was standing in a car park having the most important conversation of my career.'
- 'A massive difference exists between what *[job title]* does on paper, and what we actually do all day. Let me explain.'

- 'The hardest transition in *[industry/career stage]* isn't learning the technical skills. It's learning how to ...'
- 'I just finished reading *Work Fame* by Leanne Hughes ...' (Extra brownie points if you use this one.)

Quick tip: You can use a version of this AI prompt to help you with crafting your opening hook:

> Write 20 opening lines for a LinkedIn post about *[topic]*. The goal is to make the first line earn the click. Use information gap theory and create curiosity without sounding clickbaity. Keep each option under 20 words. Mix these styles: surprising confession, sharp contrast, specific moment, unexpected question and bold opinion. Avoid clichés, corporate fluff and hype. Make the hooks sound like a smart human, not a copywriter trying too hard.

You can find this prompt to copy and paste in your reader toolkit at getworkfame.com/start. (And tag me @leannehughes in your first post!) Use the prompt for inspiration and to give you some ideas, but still ensure the opening line (and your post) are in your voice.

Start small. Curate an interesting article, chronicle a challenge you are working through, or create a single post with a hook that makes someone stop scrolling.

Scene 24

The thought breeder loop

This scene is about idea generation: where to find ideas, how to notice them and how to become a better observer of the world around you.

Life is filled with rich experiences — you just have to pause and notice them. That is why the Walk of Fame in scene 1 (way back at the beginning of this book) is so powerful. When you keep your head up, you become more aware of what is happening around you.

In December 2024, I created a daily podcast called *Leanne on Demand*. My goal was to draw lessons from everyday life and reflect on them through the lens of my work. Sharing and capturing these instances each day trained me to notice things I might have otherwise ignored. This is one of the great benefits of sharing your ideas publicly: it makes you more aware of what is happening around you and helps you learn and appreciate every day.

Notice, capture, shape, post

The first step is simply noticing — and this isn't about living a more interesting life. You don't need extraordinary experiences to create coverage. Everyday moments are more relatable than dramatic ones because your audience has their own versions of the same experience.

As shown in the following figure, once you've noticed something, you then just have to capture, shape and post it.

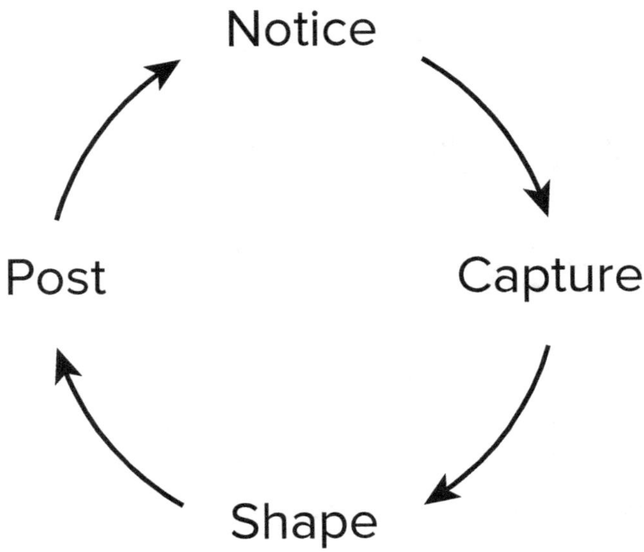

The *Work Fame* thought breeder loop

Notice

Pay attention when something catches your attention, such as a comment in a meeting that made you think, a pattern you've spotted across different projects, a question someone asked that brought out a strong opinion or a podcast episode that triggered a reaction. Even a problem you solved this week that someone else is probably facing right now counts. Thought breeders notice what makes them pause, lean in or disagree.

Here's how you can find inspiration:

- Keep your head up and notice what grabs your interest.
- If you pause to take a photo, ask yourself why you did, and turn that 'why' into something you can share.

- If a conversation sticks with you or a particular phrase stays in your mind after a meeting, try to share that insight in your own words.
- If you're screenshotting something on your phone, again ask yourself why and how it might be useful. Anything that makes you pause, take note, lean in or feel something strongly can serve as raw material for your coverage.

Capture

Noticing ideas and inspiration is great, but becoming someone who's great at capturing ideas before they disappear is key. So many times, I've thought, *Oh, that's such a good idea, I'll remember that!* and a few minutes later, it's gone.

I'm not going to prescribe the best tool for capturing ideas, but I will say two key things make a great idea repository:

1. It must be within reach through the day (inspiration doesn't follow a schedule).
2. It must be the easiest thing for you to use.

For me, I just use the Notes app on my phone and write a quick note to myself, tagged with #Idea. That makes it easy to search. My phone is always with me, it syncs across devices and I can search it.

Otherwise, you can also try:

- *Voice notes:* Open your voice memo app, talk through the idea as if you're explaining it to a friend and save it. You can get a transcript later and shape it from there. This is also faster than typing when you're on the move.
- *A dedicated capture app:* Tools such as Notion or even a simple spreadsheet work well if you want more structure. You might like to categorise your ideas by theme or pillar as you go.

- *Screenshots:* When you see a post, an article headline, a quote or anything that sparks a reaction, screenshot it. Create a folder on your phone called 'Ideas' and dump them there.
- *A physical notebook:* You might think better on paper. If that's you, keep a small notebook in your bag. I find a notebook works well when you wake up in the middle of the night with the 'best idea ever' but don't want to ruin your sleep with the blue light from your phone.

Shape

An idea in your Notes app is just a thought. To make it valuable to someone else, you need to shape it. This is where you transition from consuming information to creating value.

Shaping is about taking the raw capture and asking, 'Why does this matter and who is it for?' You are translating your personal observation into a professional insight. If you captured a frustrated thought about a clunky meeting, for example, shaping it means pulling out the lesson on how to run a better one. If you saved a screenshot of a quote you loved, shaping it means adding a specific example of how you applied that quote in your work this week.

As you shape, tighten the phrases. Remove the corporate jargon. Add a specific, real-world example to ground the concept. The best test is then to read it out loud. If you wouldn't say those words to a colleague while waiting for a coffee, rewrite it.

Post

Hit publish before you feel 100 per cent ready. If you feel a bit uncomfortable, that's a good sign — it means you're not playing too safe. After you've posted, close the app and get on with your day. Check in once or twice to respond to any comments but also remember that the notifications (or lack of) are not a reflection on you!

Dealing with comments

Let's talk about comments. Ideally, you want to start a conversation on LinkedIn because the platform tends to reward posts that get real interaction, which means more eyeballs on your post. That said, you can handle this in different ways, especially when you're starting out.

At first, you might want to 'post and run', which is how I started. I shared something online and then avoided looking at it for the rest of the day. But I recognise now that comments are really useful — they show you what people are curious about and confused by, what they agree with and what has hit a nerve. That's gold.

Also keep in mind that, early on, most of your comments will probably come from people in your existing network. These are people who know you and support you, or are at least interested enough to join in. So, if someone takes the time to leave a thoughtful comment, reply.

Now, what if someone challenges you? First, don't panic. A challenge is often a sign that you have said something interesting enough for someone to react — so if someone pushes back, re-read their comment. They might be right, they might have misunderstood you or they might have added a fresh perspective to consider. Or they might just be projecting! Again, remember to separate yourself from the idea.

If a comment fires you up, don't reply straightaway. Step away, make a cup of tea, walk around the block or at the very least type your response somewhere else first. Let it cool. If needed, send your response to a trusted friendtor and ask for their feedback.

Finally, remember that not every comment needs a big response — some comments deserve a proper reply, while others just need a quick thank you or some clarification.

Scene 25

Landing speaking opportunities

When someone is standing at the front of a room speaking to you, they have a kind of built-in authority. You didn't give this authority to them consciously; it just happens. They were invited to speak, so your brain assigns them status before they have said a single word.

If you're the one speaking in front of a room, you're also granted this built-in authority. It also puts you in front of people outside your usual circle who might deeply resonate with your message. It forces you to clarify your own thinking and storytelling, making you a sharper communicator in your day job. As a professional, this may be one of the rare moments in your working life when people genuinely stop, pay attention and listen to what you have to say.

And, as a bonus, if the session gets recorded, you will also have content you can share for months afterwards.

Why speak?

Becoming an in-demand speaker or presenter isn't the focus of this book, but speaking is a powerful way to charge all three spotlights at once.

Speaking opens doors, puts you in interesting places and introduces you to people who might never have heard of you. When your message resonates, it draws the right people to you and positions you as someone worth listening to.

It also builds confidence for high stakes work moments. Speaking to strangers in unfamiliar settings develops new skills. That discomfort helps your growth and self-development.

Speaking broadens your network, too, and particularly with people in your industry. Every event you speak at connects you with organisers, fellow speakers and audience members who share your interests. Those relationships compound.

Start small

My first speaking experience outside of work was at PechaKucha (Japanese for 'chit-chat'), a community event format where you present 20 slides for 20 seconds each, for a total of six minutes and 40 seconds. My topic was about running my first marathon, which had nothing to do with my job. I was simply telling a story that I thought my local community might find interesting. Hosting lunch and learns (scene 17) is a great option for a similar reason — getting comfortable with speaking in smaller groups.

Talking to my local community then gave me the confidence to apply for my first industry speaking opportunity: DisruptHR, with a similar format of 15 slides and speaking for 20 seconds for each slide. That one talk changed my trajectory. I met a terrific lifelong friend at that event and, afterwards, connected with people on LinkedIn who have been following my work for years.

Before DisruptHR, I thought only experts with lots of credentials could get on stage. But the organisers cared more about my topic's relevance than my credentials. My job role provided credibility and my company's name certainly helped but, ultimately, the topic did the heavy lifting — and you too can generate topic ideas that link closely to conference themes.

That's really all you need — a useful perspective and a topic that immediately grabs the organiser's interest, based on their audience.

What makes a topic land?

A lot of speaking applications blend into the pile because they sound like everything else — 'Leadership in a changing world', for example, 'Building high-performing teams' or 'Navigating digital transformation'.

Most conferences have a theme, and it's important to figure out how you can weave that theme into your topic and make it stand out. Every industry (or the world, like with AI right now) also has trends that draw attention.

What I like to do is take out a piece of paper, write down the conference theme and what's trending in my industry, and then reflect on my work experiences. What stories, projects or challenges link to these themes? Drawing out a mind map also helps.

When you land on some key ideas, remember to give your presentation a great title!

When Adam Mustoe and I spoke at the Global CliftonStrengths Summit in Omaha, our topic was 'The seven attributes of superhero facilitators'. This was specific, fun and mixed our perspectives.

Quick tip: Collaborating with someone whose expertise complements yours can be a great way to get a start speaking. Chat to your friendtors about this idea!

I talk about how important the title is when outlining how to run your first lunch and learn session in scene 17, so flick back if you need some further inspiration.

Finding opportunities

Your professional association is the easiest starting point when looking for speaking opportunities. Every profession has associations, and they run events that need speakers. Get involved, show up to their events first and pay attention to what gaps you could fill.

Also keep an eye on industry conferences, which announce speaker calls months in advance. Use AI tools to track conferences and set alerts for open submissions.

If you're planning to attend an industry conference as a guest anyway, apply to speak first. If you get selected, brilliant. If not, you have lost nothing, and you can still attend as an attendee. While you're there, pay attention to what connects with the audience and who is organising the event. Those connections are your path in for next time.

Want to uplevel all of this? Get in touch with the event organisers directly. Send them a short video introducing yourself, explaining why you're excited about the event and giving them a taste of who you are as a presenter. A 60-second video that shows your energy and lets them hear your voice will do more for your application than an extra paragraph of bio text ever could.

At a base level, associations and events usually list the office bearers and event organisers on their website, so make sure you connect with them on LinkedIn.

Awards and recognition programs

Look for awards in your industry that recognise projects, teams or individuals. Many professional associations, industry bodies and trade publications run annual programs or awards nights that are actively looking for entries.

Your organisation may also have internal recognition programs worth nominating yourself or a colleague for.

The act of applying for such awards is valuable in itself. Writing an award submission forces you to articulate the impact of your work in clear, compelling terms (everything you've been working on in this book).

If you're shortlisted or win, you have a credible, third-party endorsement of your work that you can share publicly and reference for years.

Quick tip: Keep a running list of relevant awards in your industry and set a reminder to check submission deadlines each year.

One talk becomes five opportunities

One speaking gig can drive Work Fame for weeks if used intentionally and be the source of more opportunities. Here's how to make the most of it:

- *Before your event, post about it:* Share your speaking topic, reasons for participating and what you hope to learn. Tag the event and organisers.
- *At the event, ask someone to capture photos or short video clips:* Behind-the-scenes moments, such as sound checks or pre-talk nerves, are often more engaging than polished stage photos.
- *Afterwards, write a reflection post about your surprises:* Create quote graphics, tag speakers and promptly connect with new contacts. One talk, shared intentionally, can generate weeks of content and connections.

Start by finding one industry association or conference in your field that accepts speaker submissions. Check when submissions open and jot down three specific, curiosity-sparking topics you could speak on.

Scene 26

Starting a limited series podcast

If you can record a Teams or Zoom call, upload the audio file to a website, add a title and publish it, you have a podcast. Surprised? Yes, that's all it takes!

The technical barrier to podcasting is almost zero. The real barrier is the story you're telling yourself about why you believe you're not the kind of person who starts a podcast.

I was conflicted about whether to include this scene because a podcast feels like a big move, and this book is supposed to be about practical things you can do inside your career without becoming a full-time content creator. But I had to share it, because this was the single thing that really made me Work Famous.

My story

When I started my podcast *First Time Facilitator*, I was new to running workshops. I couldn't find any podcasts on facilitation, so I made one myself.

Each recorded conversation gave me new workplace skills and extended my influence beyond internal channels. Those on my

'Quest' list were also keen to join because I shone the spotlight on them. Within a year, others were calling me a facilitation expert, even though I was still just starting out.

The podcast opened doors as colleagues and leaders noticed my extracurricular efforts and started inviting me to host a variety of internal events.

Podcasts charge every spotlight

A podcast super-charges each of your Work Fame spotlights.

Podcasts and your Contribution spotlight

Every episode you produce makes you better at your actual job. You research a topic before you record, which means you're reading and thinking more deeply than you would otherwise. You sit across from someone interesting and learn to ask sharper questions, listen more carefully and synthesise ideas on the fly. Every episode makes you a sharper thinker and a better communicator.

As researcher Michael Bossetta found when studying the professional benefits of hosting an interview podcast,

> Each stage of podcast production facilitates learning and skill acquisition. Scouting new material encourages exposure to new topics ... Preparing for an interview requires critical engagement with the work of a researcher ... recording ... helps a podcaster hone communication skills ... the main benefactor of any podcast series is ... the podcaster.[20]

That has been my experience too. The *First Time Facilitator* podcast has taught me more about facilitation than any course I have ever taken.

Podcasts and your Conversations spotlight

Here is something I have learned from years of reaching out to people: if you ask someone to 'pick their brain', the chances of getting a yes are 50/50. But if you ask them to be a guest on your podcast, they will almost certainly say yes.

A podcast invitation is a completely different proposition from a vague coffee invite. You're offering them a platform. An upside exists for both of you, and your request feels generous rather than extractive. That is why podcasting is such a powerful Conversations spotlight charger. It gives you a reason to contact people on your Quest list and a format that makes it easy for them to say yes.

Your guests might also recommend others or you might say, 'Hey, can you introduce me to so-and-so?' That expands your Quest network even more.

Podcasts and your Coverage spotlight

Every episode you publish is a piece of your thinking that keeps working after you've moved on. It sits online — findable, shareable and building your reputation while you sleep. When someone asks me a great question, I'll often turn it into a podcast episode because I know other people are wondering the same thing. One conversation becomes a resource that hundreds of people find over months and years. That is what Coverage looks like at its best: your perspective, published once, delivering value on repeat.

Also, a neat perk of podcast hosting? Once you have a show, people start inviting you to speak. You become someone with a platform, and that changes how organisers and conference committees see you.

Have I convinced you yet? C'mon — schedule your first virtual call and launch your limited series podcast.

Your 90-day project

I'm not suggesting you commit to a weekly show. When I was an employee, maintaining a weekly podcast alongside a full-time job was tough. Scheduling conversations is hard. So, here's the low-pressure version: a limited series with five to ten episodes. This is a 90-day project with a clear start and finish. Saying, 'I am going to record seven conversations about *[topic]* over the next three months' feels completely manageable, while saying, 'I am starting a podcast' feels like a life sentence. The limited series removes that pressure entirely.

To create your limited series, start by picking a topic that genuinely interests you. Next, make a list of five to seven people you'd like to interview on this theme. Then schedule and record these conversations over the next few months.

For structure, I suggest about ten episodes. Six or seven should be interviews with experts or people you admire from your Quest list. Also include your own solo takes: an introduction episode where you set up the series, a halfway episode reflection on what you're learning and a final episode about what the whole series taught you. This is enough to stamp your authority.

Once recorded, publish the episodes online and let them remain accessible for others — people and AI will be able to find them long after you've completed the series, giving your work lasting impact.

I had a weekly interview-style podcast and that was tough, but I did my daily podcast *Leanne on Demand* for a whole year because it was just a five-minute voice note. What you can do really depends on the structure. In the context of this book, I suggest interviews that are no longer than 30 minutes each, which makes it manageable for you and your guests.

Topic choice

When considering your topic choice, choose what you want to be famous for. What are the areas you want to grow in? Don't necessarily consider something you're already an expert on right now, because that can get boring unless you're doing it as a legacy project to capture what you know. This is about moving you forward and propelling you to where you want to go.

Pick a topic that really connects with you. My friend Ronsley Vaz gave me the best advice on this: create a podcast on something you want to learn more about. That curiosity is what keeps you going. It also makes you a better interviewer because you're genuinely interested, and it means every episode teaches you something you can use.

If you did the Work Fame field trip from scene 2, look at your Expect column. What did you write down as the reputation you want to build? Your podcast topic should point in that direction.

DIY your show

Start recording now with your present set-up — don't let technical doubts hold you back.

The hosting available is cheap and some platforms offer free tiers. Editing is also a lot easier with tools such as Descript. (You can find out my entire podcast tech stack at getworkfame.com/start.) Once your episodes are uploaded, the hosting platform automatically distributes them to Spotify, Apple Podcasts and everywhere else.

You can also upload the video versions to YouTube and repurpose the transcripts into articles on LinkedIn or Substack. One conversation can become content across multiple platforms with very little extra effort.

You can create further content by writing about lessons learned from each episode and publishing those as articles or posts. You can grab quotes from your guests and turn them into LinkedIn posts that tag them, which opens relationships and puts your work in front of their networks, too. You can create a Substack, newsletter or blog where you host the episodes alongside written reflections. That becomes your permanent body of work, and a searchable online home for your thinking.

That's why a podcast is such a strong asset. It sits online, but you can move the content into multiple formats and platforms. One 30-minute conversation can generate weeks of coverage.

Listeners still email me about episodes recorded years ago, because the content's value lasts.

Work Fame in action

Anthony Domanti

Anthony Domanti (also known as AD) is a senior principal civil engineer and the co-host of *The Good Drop*, a podcast about water engineering.

AD started the podcast because his good friend and colleague of 12 years, Simon Hawkes, was leaving the company they worked at together. AD wanted to overcome a bad habit of losing friendships due to work relocations, and instead stay in contact. They came up with the idea of doing a podcast together about the water industry—and it has been a game changer.

The Good Drop is framed as a journey down the river of water engineering. They don't pump out episodes every week (pun intended); instead, they record when they have the time and when it works for them. They interview people from across the industry, but the conversations go much deeper than technical specs. They talk about resilience, fear, failure and continual improvement. The water industry has a lot of amazing people, and they feel it's great to 'tap' into them and learn from them.

The impact of the podcast has been massive. AD says it hasn't just changed his career; it has also changed his life. Professionally, the opportunities and networks made have been incredible. After interviewing the CEO of a Swiss pump company, for example, (after an initial connection made over a massive block of Toblerone at a water event), AD was invited to Switzerland to tour their factory as a guest. A similar opportunity was realised from a managing director of a Swedish pump supplier after hearing one of episodes of *The Good Drop*.

AD believes the production of the podcast was also one of the primary reasons he was named the Australian Water Association's Queensland Water Professional of the Year in 2023. From the podcast, he has evolved from 'Anthony the engineer' to 'AD the

(*continued*)

artist', a recognised voice championing growth and change in the industry.

When I asked him how he manages the time commitment on top of a demanding day job, he admitted that editing takes up a bit of time per episode, but he's recently started using AI to handle the post-interview editing, which has made the process more efficient. Because it's a labour of love and they only release episodes when it suits them, it never feels like a burden.

His advice for anyone thinking about starting a podcast? 'Just go for it. You've got to have a good reason and the passion of creating a podcast, so it doesn't become a chore. But it's been a wonderful experience—it really has opened windows, doors and opportunities.'

The private podcast

If a public show seems too much, start a private podcast for your organisation.

A private podcast is a series locked down to your organisation, shared via a link on your SharePoint or intranet and listenable through the same podcast apps your colleagues already use. I use a tool called Hello Audio for creating private podcasts.

Think about the last time your organisation recorded a town hall or a webinar. That recording probably lives on SharePoint right now. How many people have watched the replay? I would suggest almost nobody. Watching a 60-minute webinar replay requires you to sit at your desk and give it your full attention. No thanks! A shorter podcast-style recording is much more attractive.

Episode ideas for your organisation's podcast

Here are some ideas for episodes to get you started:

- a town hall or all-hands meeting, reformatted for audio
- a quarterly team update, shared as a podcast instead of a replay
- an interview with a leader or managing director about their career path or a challenge they navigated
- a conversation with an external expert on a topic your team is wrestling with
- a 'lessons from the field' episode where a colleague shares how they solved a real problem
- a roundtable with people from different regions or teams on a shared challenge
- a 'new starter' episode, covering what someone wishes they had known in their first 90 days
- a spotlight on a project, outlining what the team set out to do, what happened and what they learnt
- an interview with a client or stakeholder about what they love about and need from your team
- a 'what's changing in our industry' episode with someone who is close to the trends
- a behind-the-scenes look at how a key decision was made
- a recurring series where different team members share one thing they are reading, testing or thinking about.

Turning content into a podcast

Once you've found an area to cover, put that content into a podcast format. Suddenly, people can listen while they are commuting or getting their 10 000 steps in during the day. Private podcast listeners consistently get better engagement than webinar replays. People don't mind longer-form audio because they can do other things at the same time as listening. You can also put your quarterly team meetings on a private podcast, producing better listen rates with the same content, simply in a different format.

I have made podcasts for outside organisations, helping them interview people across the business worldwide on specific topics. We have brought in external experts. We've recorded interviews with managing directors and leaders across several sites and regions. What we've quickly discovered while making these podcasts is that people throughout different parts of the business are dealing with remarkably similar challenges. The podcast then becomes a wonderful opportunity for people to share their stories, tips and how they got through a work challenge.

Hosting a podcast internally at your company opens many opportunities to chat with people and casts you as someone others listen to. It builds your status and authority in the business.

Spotlight check: Coverage

Coverage is where Work Fame travels—it is what carries your ideas, your name and your thinking beyond the people who already know you.

This part of the book has been about getting clearer on what you want to say, closing the gap between the expertise you have and the visibility you hold, and building a habit of sharing that feels sustainable rather than performative.

Rate this spotlight

On a scale of 1 to 10, how bright is your Coverage spotlight right now? Rate yourself based on the following:

- *1:* I have ideas, but I mostly keep them to myself and overthink everything.
- *10:* I know what I want to talk about, I have a visible point of view, and I share my thinking in ways that feel natural and sustainable.

Write your number down. What would it look like if you were one to two points higher? What would you do differently?

Three questions to reflect on

Consider the following questions to reflect on your Coverage spotlight:

1. *What idea are you still sitting on for no good reason?* What is the smallest possible version of it you could share this week—perhaps a single sentence, a short post or a comment on someone else's thread?
2. *What story do you keep telling yourself about why you're not ready to post, write, speak or share?* What is the cost of waiting until you feel ready?
3. *If someone looked you up today, what evidence would they find of how you think?* What's the one thing you wish they could see that isn't there yet?

Share the spotlight

Work Fame sounds great when you work in a healthy workplace with a supportive boss, a decent culture and enough breathing room to think strategically. But let's be real — a lot of people are trying to build a reputation inside systems that are messy, political and under-resourced, and with toxic cultures.

So, in this part, I take you through some common workplace dilemmas, such as your boss blocking your spotlights, a lack of opportunities where you work or you not feeling the extrovert life is for you. I then offer some tips and advice for leading your team's and your organisation's Work Fame.

Scene 27

Work Fame dilemmas

Let's chat about a few of the objections that might still be rattling around in your head, even after working through the three Work Fame spotlights.

'What if my boss is a roadblock?'

This is one of the big ones. Maybe your boss keeps everything close. Maybe they don't advocate for you. Maybe they don't like you getting visibility outside the team because it makes them feel exposed, threatened or out of control.

First, don't gaslight yourself. Some managers are blockers, and not every problem in your career is a mindset issue. People typically leave bosses, not organisations. However, even in this situation, you still have options available to you. You don't need your manager's permission to become more useful, clearer or better connected. You may need to be more tactical, but you're not powerless.

Start by becoming easier to advocate for, even if they are not naturally good at it. Give them receipts. Give them crisp updates they can forward. Give them language. Make it ridiculously easy for them to repeat your value upwards.

Then, open a side door — look around your organisation to see if other leaders or teams might fit your career aspirations better. Build strong relationships with peers, adjacent teams, project leads and people who can speak about your work from experience. Start reconnecting with old colleagues working in other organisations.

You might also start asking whether this environment deserves your best years.

'What if my work has no opportunities?'

Two situations are possible here. The first is that opportunities exist, but you just don't know about them yet — or you may have typecast yourself, and more ways to transfer your skills are available than you have considered. This is especially true in larger organisations. The bigger the company, the more projects, committees, secondments and cross-functional initiatives that are running at any given time.

In a smaller business, the honest reality is that fewer of these opportunities pop up, and that's worth acknowledging. But even in a small team, you can usually find ways to stretch; volunteering for something outside your usual remit, for example, connecting with people in adjacent industries or building your reputation externally so that opportunities come to you from outside the organisation.

The second possibility is that there genuinely is not much room to grow where you are. Still, remember that growth is not only upward. Moving laterally within a business can make you more well-rounded and open doors that a straight vertical climb would not.

Before you declare the cupboard empty, ask yourself:

- 'Have I raised this with my manager? What's their response?'
- 'What have I put my hand up for?'
- 'Who have I spoken to outside my team?'

If you've really checked and your workplace is a dead end, be honest about it. Now is a good time to build your reputation outside your organisation so you have more options when you are ready to move, and moving might be exactly the right call. If the environment genuinely cannot give you what you need, there is no shame in finding one that can.

Otherwise, you can try to bring back that spark by creating your own project, such as a limited series podcast, a newsletter or a speaking topic you pitch to an industry event — these are things you can build regardless of where you work or what your job title says.

'What if I hate what I do?'

Oooh ... If you hate what you do? Becoming famous for work you resent really is no fun. That's why we went through the Drain/Gain exercise back in scene 2, and part of that was identifying what specifically drains you and why.

Hating your work is not a small thing, and trying to become more visible in a role that drains you can feel pointless — or, worse, like you're cementing yourself into something you're desperate to leave.

If you dislike your work, use the Contribution spotlight in a new way. Don't just focus on your current role. Instead, get clear on what drains you, what energises you and what you want to be known for next.

Then start shifting your reputation in that direction through small actions that draw you closer to your strengths. Take on different projects, engage in different conversations, contribute different coverage and participate in different rooms.

You don't need to blow up your life tomorrow. But you do need to stop reinforcing the identity you're trying to leave.

Also, I'd recommend reading *Pivot: The Only Move That Matters Is Your Next One* by Jenny Blake. It's very helpful if you're considering a career change.

The goal here is to use the tools in this book to move toward work that fuels you.

'What if I'm not an extrovert?'

Thoughtful. Prepared. Consistent. Generous. These are not extrovert traits — they are Work Famous traits. Some of the most Work Famous people I know are introverts, and several are featured in this book. They ask good questions, follow up, host well, write clearly and are highly analytical.

The assumption behind this question is that getting recognition requires you to be loud — but the difference with Work Fame is that it requires you to be useful and share value, and usefulness has nothing to do with how much energy you get from a networking event.

Look at the three spotlights. Contribution is about the quality and clarity of your work. Conversations is about building real relationships, which introverts often do brilliantly because they listen well and follow through. Coverage is about sharing your thinking through your preferred medium, which could simply be writing. Every spotlight can be lit up in a way that suits how you're wired.

The book is also designed with multiple entry points. You don't have to start by speaking at a town hall. You can start by commenting on someone's post, running a listening tour one coffee at a time or writing a short internal update that highlights your team's work. These are quiet, deliberate moves, and they compound just as powerfully as the loud ones.

Being Work Famous is a practice. And introverts often do it well because they tend to be more intentional, more prepared and more genuinely curious about the people around them.

What every person I have featured in this book does well is voluntarily push themselves beyond their comfort zone, which is different from pretending to be an extrovert. Being Work Famous is a set of behaviours, and you get to choose the ones that fit you.

'What if I've been overlooked for years?'

If you feel like you've been overlooked at work, you need to stop hoping that one perfect move will fix everything. When people have an old idea about you, you change it by showing new evidence over time, not with one big moment.

I've felt this too, and one of the most effective ways I've found to cut through it is to stop waiting for internal recognition and go get external recognition instead. Apply for industry awards — it's completely fine to self-nominate. Use the Coverage spotlight to build your reputation outside your organisation. Speak at an event. Start writing. You might be surprised to find that once the outside world starts noticing you, the inside world catches up.

Here are some other ideas to help you move forward:

- *Go to reputation rehab:* Start a concentrated effort over 90 days at completing some of the scenes in this book.
- *Look at changing roles:* Consider working with another manager or team in your existing workplace.
- *Start over:* Once an identity is ingrained, resetting it can be difficult, and even harder when you work in an environment that might reinforce it.

Quick tip: Some of the dilemmas in this scene might be reasons to look for other opportunities. A helpful question might be, 'Given my situation, what version of Work Fame makes sense for me right now?'

'What if I can't post about my work?'

Not being able to post about their organisation is a real constraint for a lot of people. If you work in government, defence, law, financial services, health care or any heavily regulated industry, strict rules often apply to what you can and cannot share publicly. Some organisations have social media policies that require approval before posting. Some roles involve confidential client work that simply cannot be discussed, and in some workplace cultures posting online is not the norm.

First, check what you actually can and can't do. Don't assume you can't post anything publicly when the reality is more nuanced. The restriction is often on sharing client information, internal data or anything commercially sensitive, not on sharing your professional perspective or ideas. Read your organisation's social media policy (if one exists) or have a direct conversation with your manager or communications team.

If the restrictions are genuine, there's still good news: Work Fame has never required you to post about your work specifically. It requires you to share your thinking. Those are two different things.

You can write about the ideas that interest you in your field without referencing anything confidential. You can share what you are reading, what you are learning and what questions you are sitting with. You can comment on industry trends, respond to other people's posts or share your perspective on a challenge your sector is grappling with. None of that requires you to reveal what you do day-to-day.

Think about it this way: a lawyer can't share details of a client matter, but they can absolutely write about how they think about a particular area of law. A government employee can't reveal policy deliberations, but they can write about the skills, frameworks or experiences that have shaped how they work.

If even that feels too exposed, remember that Coverage is just one of the three spotlights. You can build significant Work Fame through Contribution and Conversations by doing excellent work, building strong relationships (both at your company and externally), and becoming the person people think of when an opportunity arises.

Scene 28

Leading your team's Work Fame

Everything in this book so far has focused on energising yourself — looking at your Contribution, your Conversations and your Coverage. If you've worked through the activities, you possess the tools, frameworks and confidence to cultivate a professional reputation that can unlock opportunities. Now, you can start helping others build their Work Fame, too.

Think about what a great celebrity agent does. They find talent, create opportunities, connect their clients with the right people, negotiate on their behalf and ensure everyone recognises their clients' talent.

If you're a leader, you do the same — identify talent, create opportunities and support your team members' career growth.

Your team's reputation reflects your leadership

Work Fame is not just for individuals; teams have reputations too. Each department or project group is known for something in the company.

When your team hosts a lunch and learn, presents at meetings, shares project wins or connects across the company, for example, they build both personal and team reputation. Repeated contributions make your team more visible.

Supporting your team's reputation is also a smart strategy for long-term success. When people feel seen and valued for their unique contributions, their connection to the work — and to you as a leader — deepens.

A large-scale Gallup workplace survey found that employees who don't feel adequately recognised are twice as likely to say they plan to leave within the year. Conversely, when leaders actively champion their team's visibility, it builds loyalty and engagement.[21] In this sense, Work Fame and public recognition aren't just 'soft' leadership gestures or nice-to-haves — they are critical retention tools. By shining a spotlight on your team, you are actively protecting your best talent.

Disclaimer: You can't make people do these things. You can encourage and support them, but they need to want it themselves.

Give your team permission

Your team might hold back on building their Work Fame until they feel it is safe to do so. They are watching you. When you talk openly about visibility, encourage them to connect outside the team and celebrate someone posting on LinkedIn, they'll follow your lead.

You can start right away. Share this book in a team meeting. Ask your team what they want to be known for. Share your own stories, including what worked and what was hard. When they see you taking action, they'll feel encouraged to join in.

The following sections outline some ideas on how you can charge their spotlights.

Contribution

Try the following to boost your team's Contribution spotlight:

- Say thank you.
- Give them stretch assignments.
- Encourage them to ask questions at business meetings.
- Send them on a listening tour.
- Invite them to present to the leadership team rather than doing it yourself.
- Recommend your team members for cross-team projects.
- Broadcast it publicly when someone delivers great work.
- Ask your team what's different between the work they do now and the work they want to be known for.

Conversations

Here are some ways to charge your team's Conversations spotlight:

- Suggest they join a friendtoring group — a small circle of peers at a similar career stage who support and challenge each other.
- Ask them to invite colleagues from other parts of the business for a coffee.
- Encourage them to host a lunch and learn, or kick off the next team call.
- Introduce your team members to people in your network who could help them.

Coverage

Finally, increase the team's Coverage spotlight with the following:

- When a team member shares something online, engage with it. Like or comment on their post. These small actions show the whole team that you value and celebrate their efforts.
- Give recommendations for your team members and tag them in posts.
- Nominate team members for industry awards.
- Share industry conferences and encourage them to speak as presenters.
- Consider a regular fame check-in.

Quick tip: You can also share the Work Fame Scorecard from the end of this book and have everyone rate themselves. Ask each person to share one action they took in the last three months to boost their profile.

This approach turns building a reputation from a solo effort into something your team does together. It builds accountability, sparks new ideas and gives quieter team members a safe space to talk with support from others.

Scene 29

Work Fame for organisations

What if you could boost the Work Fame spotlights and build the reputation of an entire organisation? Imagine hundreds (or thousands) of people inside a company, all building their Work Fame at the same time. Think about all these people telling stories about their work, connecting across departments and becoming visible in their industries. Your organisation might be sitting on a brilliant, untapped marketing channel: the people already on your payroll.

How one global company built 6000 internal influencers

Sanofi is a global pharmaceutical company with around 80 000 employees. For years, the unwritten rule in the company was simple: don't post anything online. In a heavily regulated industry, silence felt like the safest option. Then their Chief Talent Officer decided to challenge that. She had seen a version of increasing employee visibility work at a previous company and knew a better way was possible. The question was not, 'Should our people be visible?' It was, 'How do we make it safe and rewarding for them to be visible?'

Anne Adam, who leads the program within Sanofi's employer branding team, told me how the team started small. They worked closely with their communications and compliance teams to build guardrails on social media posts. Instead of a blanket 'don't post' policy, they created clear guidance on what employees could talk about and how to do it confidently. Then they piloted the changes with a small group of people who were already active on social media — employees who just needed permission and a bit of structure.

The real turning point came when the company sponsored the Paris 2024 Olympic Games. Thousands of Sanofi employees went to Paris as volunteers, torch bearers and spectators. It was a significant investment in employee engagement, and it was also the perfect moment to train people in storytelling and visibility. The team upskilled these employees and brought them into what they call the Sanofi Influencer Community.

Within two years, the community grew to over 6000 members across every business unit, every function and every level of seniority, from interns to senior executives.

Why people showed up

Those 6000 employees didn't join the community because they were told to. Nothing in this program is mandatory — if you sign up, you don't need to post a certain number of posts per month. But community members continue to show up to the monthly workshops because the program is built on a genuine win–win.

The individual gains the chance to build their Work Fame, grow a professional network, develop storytelling skills and increase their own visibility. In a world where AI is making CVs look increasingly similar, a nurtured online presence is one of the few ways to genuinely stand out.

For the organisation, the impact is enormous.

The community's posts have reached over 33 million people in a single year (a conservative figure) and those are not random eyeballs. Every employee's network is made up of former colleagues, people with similar skills and professionals in the same industry. When your people post, they are reaching exactly the talent pools you want to be visible in. No paid media campaign can replicate that kind of targeted, trusted reach.

Sanofi's employer brand strengthened too, according to LinkHumans' Employer Brand Index, a quarterly measure of how people were talking about the company across platforms such as LinkedIn and Glassdoor. The narrative shifted because real employees were telling real stories. That will always be more compelling than anything a corporate channel can produce.

The stories that prove it works

One employee in the program became so active on LinkedIn that he connected with a former speechwriter from the White House (what a perk!). Another employee told the team, 'I get stopped in the elevator now. People say they loved my post. I don't even know who they are'.

But my favourite story is about a woman in Paris who had been working with the company for almost 30 years. She said the program gave her something she had never had before: a place for her voice. She felt, for the first time, that she could express herself creatively and professionally.

This is not a marketing initiative dressed up as employee engagement. It is genuine professional development that happens to produce extraordinary business results.

Adopting Work Fame in your organisation

If you're reading this and thinking about building something similar inside your organisation, here are the principles that make the difference:

- *Start with permission:* The regulatory and compliance groundwork must come first. People need to feel safe before they will feel brave. Work with your comms and legal teams to create clear, simple guidelines that tell people what they can do, not just what they cannot.
- *Pilot with your naturals:* Find the people who are already somewhat active on social media or interested. Let them be your proof of concept. Their early success will attract others far more effectively than any internal campaign.
- *Make it genuinely useful for the individual:* If the program only benefits the company, people will see through it instantly. Every workshop, every resource and every challenge must answer the question: what is in it for them? The answer should include storytelling skills, career development, personal brand growth and a stronger professional network — real value that travels with them regardless of where their career goes next.
- *Make it fun:* Sanofi runs monthly workshops, creates AI-powered content prompts, builds templates people can personalise and designs challenges with real incentives. When they needed 12 people to participate in a team event with their McLaren Formula One partnership, they turned it into a competition: the 12 Paris-based influencers with the most engagement that month won the spots. The incentive doesn't need to be that grand, it just needs to be meaningful to your people.

Both you and your organisation win

When your employees build their Work Fame, the benefit does not stop with the individual. Yes, they become better known, more confident and more connected. But the organisation also gains something incredibly valuable: a workforce that can explain the work, share the work and carry the story of the business into places the corporate brand can't reach alone.

An internal influencer community that spans departments, functions and levels creates collaboration no org chart could design. People discover colleagues they would not otherwise have met and learn about projects happening in other parts of the business.

The external results are powerful too. When employees share useful, credible stories about their work, the organisation reaches more of the right people: future employees, customers, partners, industry peers and advocates. That's why employee-led storytelling can strengthen the employer brand and build market trust.

When employees aspire to be known for great work, the organisation becomes known for the great work its people are doing.

The result is a win on three levels: individuals build reputations that support their careers, teams become more connected across silos, and the organisation earns a more human, trusted and expansive reputation in the market.

Conclusion

Your Work Fame starts now

Back in scene 1, I encouraged you to adopt a Walk of Fame and asked you to greet a stranger. Now I'd like you to take a moment and greet yourself.

You picked up a book with 'fame' on the cover because you wanted more from your career. When you started reading, you might have believed that good work speaks for itself, that being visible feels awkward or that this kind of thing is only for extroverts and self-promoters. I hope every page since then has changed your mind.

Work Fame is built through service. It's built by doing work worth noticing, and then making sure it gets noticed. The good news is that Contribution, Conversations and Coverage are skills that you can learn, practice and get better at, no matter where you are in your career or what kind of person you are.

The people you met in this book prove it. They weren't born with some special confidence gene. They simply decided to act or said yes before they felt ready. They raised their hand, started a conversation, shared an idea or simply wore a tie on a Tuesday. You can do something similar, starting today.

Don't put this book on a shelf and forget about everything you've learned. Choose one action and commit to it now. Reconnect with someone you've lost touch with, book a coffee with a colleague outside your team, or volunteer for a project that stretches you. Share one idea publicly, whether that's on LinkedIn, in a meeting or wherever you feel brave enough to start.

What you're building isn't tied to your current role or your current company. Work Fame is a career asset that travels with you. The relationships you build now will open doors years from now. The presence you create will help carry you through every restructure, every leadership change and every career pivot. You will never have to start from zero.

I'd absolutely love to hear your stories—including the projects, promotions, perks and Walk of Fame moments you didn't see coming. Send them to me at hello@leannehughes.com.

Now go. Head up, headphones out. I'll see you on the Walk of Fame.

Additional resources

I've provided here some resources to get you acting straightaway and find a quick fix if one of your spotlights needs a boost.

Your 90-day Work Fame action plan

Work Fame builds through small, consistent moves across all three spotlights. This 90-day plan gives you one focused month per spotlight, and then brings them together in the final stretch.

Before you start: Pick your target

Take five minutes to answer these questions before starting your 90-day plan:

- 'What do I want to be known for in 90 days?'
- 'Which spotlight needs the most charge right now: Contribution, Conversations or Coverage?'
- 'What's one opportunity I want to create or be considered for?'

Write your answers down. Come back to them at day 30 and day 60.

Remember — you don't have to do everything on this 90-day plan. Pick two or three actions per spotlight each month and do those well. If you want to know which spotlight to prioritise first, access the free Work Fame Scorecard at the end of this book.

Days 1–30: Set the stage

The goal this month is clarity. Know what you want to be known for, who's already in your corner and what people find when they look you up.

Contribution

- ☐ Write your 'famous for' sentence — one clear line that captures what you want to be known for.
- ☐ Start a Work Receipts folder and add your first three entries.
- ☐ Identify one strength you want to attach to your name this quarter.

Conversations

- ☐ List 15 warm-but-dormant contacts from your Best and Test groups.
- ☐ Reach out to three of these contacts with a specific, genuine message, or value share.
- ☐ Book two coffees, calls or walk and talks.

Coverage

- ☐ Audit what people find when they look you up online.
- ☐ Update your photo, headline and summary on LinkedIn so they reflect who you are now.
- ☐ Capture ten raw observations, ideas or things you've learned recently.

Days 31–60: Step into the spotlight

The goal this month is action. Start showing up in rooms, sharing your thinking and making your work visible to people beyond your immediate team.

Contribution

- ☐ Use the language your organisation cares about in an update, proposal or presentation.
- ☐ Present a piece of work in a clearer, more structured format than usual.
- ☐ Name one risk or objection in a meeting before someone else does.

Conversations

- ☐ Host something — a lunch and learn, a team debrief or a small cross-functional session.
- ☐ Ask a question at a town hall, all-hands or senior meeting where you'd usually stay quiet.
- ☐ Reconnect with three more people from your connections list.

Coverage

- ☐ React thoughtfully to five people's posts or pieces of work this month.
- ☐ Leave a specific, considered comment on someone's work or idea.
- ☐ Turn one real work moment into a short post or observation you share publicly.

Days 61–90: Keep the cameras rolling

The goal this month is compounding. Pull your work receipts together, go after a stretch opportunity and make sure the right people know what you've been doing.

Contribution

- ☐ Ask for or create one stretch opportunity that puts you in front of new people.
- ☐ Share a specific result with confidence — name what you did and why it mattered.
- ☐ Pull together three strong proof points (or Work Receipts) ready for your next review, pitch or conversation.

Conversations

- ☐ Follow up with every meaningful contact from the past 60 days.
- ☐ Invite one interesting person into your world for a coffee, an intro or a collaboration.
- ☐ Put your hand up for a panel, event or internal session.

Coverage

- ☐ Publish something with a clearer, more specific point of view than before.
- ☐ Pitch a speaking spot, internal session or guest contribution somewhere new.
- ☐ Build one reusable visibility asset — a one-pager, a template or a talk you can repeat.

Work Fame quick fix

Need to boost a spotlight? Here's a quick guide to actions you can take, depending on which spotlight needs more attention and which specific scene will be most worthwhile focusing on.

Keep in mind that while I've grouped scenes by each spotlight, they can also help boost other spotlights — going on a listening tour (in your Contribution spotlight) can also boost your Conversations spotlight, for example, and moving from audience member to the hot seat of asking a question or sitting on a panel (in the Conversations spotlight) can also improve both your Contribution and Coverage spotlights.

Work Fame quick fix action

Work Fame scene	Quick action
Spotlight one: Contribution	
2. What do you want to be famous for?	Do the Work Fame field trip: spend 60 minutes away from your desk mapping what you want to be known for.
3. Rewrite your script	Do the meme exercise: write down what you think your manager and colleagues would say about you and what you do, and then ask one trusted person to do the same.
4. Going on tour	Book two 20-minute listening chats with people outside your immediate team.
5. Learning your lines	Write a two-sentence explanation of what you do and why it matters.

(continued)

Work Fame quick fix action (*cont'd*)

Work Fame scene	**Quick action**
6. Every day is an audition	Choose one meeting this week to show up more prepared, visible and useful.
7. Giving your work a better entrance	Turn one update into a sharper format—a one-page summary or short walkthrough.
8. Save the reviews	Create a folder and save three pieces of positive feedback or proof of results.
9. Fund your fame	Spend money or time on one learning move you have been waiting for work to fund.
Spotlight two: Conversations	
10. People are people (even in the C-suite)	Identify one person you have been putting on a pedestal and plan one natural way to connect with them this month.
11. Capturing your connections	Make a list of 20 people in your professional orbit you do not want to lose touch with.
12. Finding your friendtors	Reach out to one smart peer and suggest a regular catch-up.
13. How to reach out (the right way)	Send one thoughtful message that is specific, warm and not just about asking for something.
14. From audience to panellist	Ask one question or volunteer once during a presentation instead of staying in passive audience mode.
15. The spotlight belongs to the host	Put your hand up to host, facilitate or introduce someone at your next event or meeting.
16. Hosting five-star meetings	Rewrite the purpose of your next meeting in one clear sentence before it starts.
17. Hosting a lunch and learn	Pick a topic you already know well and invite a small group to a session this month.
18. Making panels more powerful	Replace one boring panel question with something specific, unexpected and useful.
19. The conference strategy	Set three goals before your next event instead of just turning up and hoping.

Work Fame scene	Quick action
Spotlight three: Coverage	
20. The thought breeder mindset	Map yourself on the consumption–creation matrix: are you a thought bleeder, leader, reader or breeder right now?
21. The Coverage Gym	Find five people on LinkedIn whose posts always make you think and turn on their notifications.
22. Establishing your voice	Write one post or update exactly how you would say it out loud.
23. What Work Famous people reveal online	Choose one of the three posting modes—curate, create or chronicle—and do it this week.
24. The thought breeder loop	Capture three raw ideas from real work moments before they disappear.
25. Landing speaking opportunities	Make a list of five places you could pitch yourself to speak at.
26. Starting a limited series podcast	Sketch out a simple five-episode podcast idea around one clear theme.
Sharing the spotlight	
27. Work Fame dilemmas	Identify your biggest Work Fame blocker and write down one thing you can do this week that does not require anyone else's permission.
28. Leading your team's Work Fame	Name one person on your team whose Work Fame you could actively support this month and identify one specific action to help them.
29. Work Fame for organisations	Share one idea from this book with a colleague or leader in your organisation and start the conversation.

Bring Leanne (and Work Fame) to Your Team or Conference

Every great organisation has a cast of talented people who deserve a bigger spotlight.

I work with companies that want to turn their people into their greatest advocates, build cultures where visibility is encouraged rather than feared and create the kind of reputation that attracts top talent before you even post the job ad.

If that sounds like you and your company, reach out! I'd love to chat with you. Here are some ways we can work together.

The Work Fame Program

My flagship internal influencer program. I partner with you to design and launch Work Fame for your organisation — extracting the thought leadership inside your business, linking it to your vision and values, and helping your people share it at scale. The result: better talent attraction, stronger retention, more innovation and a healthier bottom line. Your people become recognised voices and your organisation becomes famous, too.

Keynote speeches

An interactive keynote speech that brings Work Fame to life for your conference, offsite or company event. High energy, high impact, and your audience leaves ready to act.

Workshops and webinars

Lunch and learn, half-day and full-day workshops built around the three spotlights. Available in person or virtually for distributed teams.

Leader sessions

A dedicated session for people leaders on how to advocate for, amplify and build a team culture where Work Fame thrives — because every star needs a great agent.

Individual and executive coaching

One-on-one coaching for high-potential leaders, executives stepping into more visible roles or anyone ready to be recognised for the work they are already doing.

Certification and licensing

Certification for internal facilitators, coaches and HR professionals who want to deliver Work Famous program content inside their organisation at scale.

Book clubs and reading groups

Download the free team discussion guide at getworkfame.com/start to access questions and prompts for each spotlight.

Say hello

Your next scene starts here. Reach out at hello@leannehughes.com or visit leannehughes.com. I can't wait to help make you, and your organisation, Work Famous.

A gift for you

The book you're holding is complete on its own — everything you need is inside. But if you'd like to go further, I've put together a free reader kit you can access at getworkfame.com/start or by scanning the QR code below.

The kit includes a Work Fame Scorecard to help you see which spotlight to focus on first, a scripts pack with ready-to-use wording for reaching out, speaking up and sharing your ideas, and a team discussion guide if you want to bring these ideas to the people you work with.

SCAN ME

Roll the credits

This book exists because of the leaders who gave me a go — the ones who said yes when I pitched a wild idea, who let me test things before I had proof they would work, and who trusted me with opportunities I had not yet earned.

Huge thanks to my dad, Aneurin Hughes, who has seen dozens of versions of this manuscript and has an eye for detail that I clearly did not inherit.

I would love to thank my early readers for dipping in and sharing their feedback: Mel Suess, Nidhi Luthra, Angela Reynolds, Nathan Mollison, Steph Clarke and Theresa Hughes. Big thanks to Jade Miller for the fab illustrations and being a book friendtor, too!

Thank you to Leigh McLennon, my publisher, for challenging my ideas and making me a better writer in the process, and to Charlotte Duff for her editing prowess.

Cheers to my local Cafe 63, which became my second home while writing this book — half of these chapters were fuelled by your coffee.

Finally, to my cosy crew. Chris, thank you — you see a side of me that the rest of the world does not, and everyone needs someone like you in their corner to support their dreams. Cheers to Quincey, my sausage dog, who sat beside me for every single writing session (except when Chris was home, because loyalty has its limits).

Notes

1. Kamel, D (2025), 'Meritocracy in workplace: Why we reward visibility over performance? Are you listening to the cackling or counting the eggs?' Available at SSRN: https://papers.ssrn.com/sol3/papers.cfm?abstract_id=5758482.
2. Harter, J & Pendell R (2025), 'Global engagement falls for the second time since 2009', Gallup Workplace, https://www.gallup.com/workplace/659279/global-engagement-falls-second-time-2009.aspx.
3. Elsbach, K, Cable, DM & Sherman, JW (2010), 'How passive "face time" affects perceptions of employees: Evidence of spontaneous trait inference', *Human Relations* 63(6), 735–760.
4. Segerstrom, SC (2007), 'Optimism and resources: Effects on each other and on health over 10 years', *Journal of Personality and Social Psychology*, 41(4), 772–786.
5. See, for example, Sagie, A & Koslowsky, M (2000), *Participation and Empowerment in Organizations*, SAGE Publications; and Back, MD, Schmukle, SC & Egloff, B (2006), 'Who is late and who is early? Big Five personality factors and punctuality attending psychological experiments', *Journal of Research in Personality*, 40(5), 841–848.
6. Ambady, N & Rosenthal, R (1992), 'Thin slices of expressive behavior as predictors of interpersonal consequences: A meta-analysis', *Psychological Bulletin*, 111(2), 256–274.

7. van Baaren, RB, Holland, RW, Steenaert, B & van Knippenberg, A (2003). 'Mimicry for money: Behavioral consequences of imitation', *Journal of Experimental Social Psychology*, 39(4), 393–398.
8. Earl, A (2025), 'Information overload: Cut through the noise for more effective internal communications', Gartner.
9. Howlett, N, Pine, K, Orakçıoğlu, İ, & Fletcher, BC (2013), 'The influence of clothing on first impressions: Rapid and positive responses to minor changes in male attire', *Journal of Fashion Marketing and Management*, 17(1), 38–48.
10. For more in this area, see Thomas, RA, West, RE & Borup, J (2017), 'An analysis of instructor social presence in online text and asynchronous video feedback comments', *The Internet and Higher Education*, 33, 61–73.
11. Nwankwo, C (2025), 'Voice notes and intimacy: Reimagining digital presence in mobile-mediated communication', University of Nigeria.
12. Dai, Y, Li, H, Xie, W & Deng, T (2022), 'Power distance belief and workplace communication: The mediating role of fear of authority', *International Journal of Environmental Research and Public Health*, 19(5), 2932.
13. Wolff, H-G & Moser, K (2009), 'Effects of networking on career success: A longitudinal study', *Journal of Applied Psychology*, 94(1), 196–206.
14. Rajkumar, K et al. (2022), 'A causal test of the strength of weak ties', *Science*, 377(6612), 1304–1310.
15. See, for example, Berger, J, Cohen, BP & Zelditch, M (1966), 'Status characteristics and expectation states', in Berger, J & Zelditch, M (eds), *Sociological Theories in Progress, Vol I*, Houghton Mifflin Company; the theory was further developed

in Berger, J, Fisek, MH, Norman, RZ & Zelditch, M (1977), *Status Characteristics and Social Interaction: An Expectation-States Approach*, Elsevier.

16. Davis, J, Wolff, H-G, Forret, ML & Sullivan, SE (2020), 'Networking via LinkedIn: An examination of usage and career benefits', *Journal of Vocational Behavior*, 118, 103396.
17. Osman, M (2025), 'Mind-blowing LinkedIn statistics and facts', Kinsta, https://kinsta.com/blog/linkedin-statistics/.
18. Mark, G (2023), *Attention Span: A Groundbreaking Way to Restore Balance, Happiness and Productivity*, HarperCollins.
19. Loewenstein, G (1994), 'The psychology of curiosity: A review and reinterpretation', *Psychological Bulletin*, 116(1), 75–98.
20. Bossetta, M (2020), 'The professional benefits of podcasting politics', *PS: Political Science & Politics*, 53(2), 328–329.
21. Gallup (2024), 'The Importance of employee recognition: Low cost, high impact', Gallup Workplace, https://gallup.com/workplace/236441/employee-recognition-low-cost-high-impact.aspx.

About Leanne

Leanne Hughes makes people famous at work.

As a keynote speaker, facilitator, adviser and author, she helps leaders and teams become more visible, influential and effective in the way they communicate and lead.

She works with organisations across many industries, including mining, aviation, pharmaceuticals and professional services, and her career has taken her from regional Australia to stages in New York, Mumbai and Mongolia.

Leanne has been recognised as Learning Professional of the Year by the Asia Pacific Institute for Learning and Performance and inducted into the Million Dollar Consulting Hall of Fame. She is the host of two podcasts, *First Time Facilitator* and *Leanne on Demand,* reaching listeners in more than 80 countries, and the author of the bestselling *The 2-Hour Workshop Blueprint*. *Work Fame* is her second book.

Her work is grounded in one belief: you do not need perfect clarity to make a meaningful move, but you do need the courage to back yourself.

Based in Brisbane, Australia, Leanne is known for blending warmth, humour and bold ideas that challenge people to think bigger and act sooner. When she is not on stage or behind a microphone, you will find her at a rooftop bar, on a Peloton or hanging out with her husband, Chris, and sausage dog, Quincey.

To book Leanne for your next event or program, visit leannehughes.com.